I'm Finally a Man

A Husband's Journey to Manhood

I'm Finally a Man

A Husband's Journey to Manhood

Demetrius & Jacqueline Irick

DeeJak's
PUBLISHING COMPANY

DeeJak's Publishing Company
Charlotte, North Carolina
www.deejakpublishingcompany.com

Printed in the United States of America

DeeJak's Publishing Company
7209- J East WT. Harris Blvd # 279
Charlotte, NC 28227-1004
www.deejakpublishingcompany.com

Editorial: Executive Dreams, CEO Rhonda Green

Cover and layout design by Perseus Design

Background design for cover: "Used with Permission from Microsoft" *Windows Server 2003 operating system, Windows is a registered trademark of Microsoft Corporation in the United States and other countries*

ISBN: 978-0-9857903-0-1 (sc)
ISBN: 978-0-9857903-2-5 (hardcover)
ISBN: 978-0-9857903-1-8 (ebook)

Library of Congress Control Number: 2012911408

Table of Contents

Acknowlegdements.. vii

Prologue ix

Introduction... xiii

The Background Story

   Chapter 1 – The Early Years......................................3

The Beginning of the End

   Chapter 2 – The Background of Self-Destruction.....11

   Chapter 3 – The Dark Side....................................... 25

   Chapter 4 – The Escape from O.B. 37

   Chapter 5 – My Addiction...41

Hell on Wheels

   Chapter 6 – My Transitional Period.........................47

   Chapter 7 – Vacation to Probation 61

   Chapter 8 – The Road to Recovery 69

I Have a New Attitude

   Chapter 9 – My Love / My Wife...............................81

Marriage Isn't Easy

   Chapter 10 – When Love Is Not Enough 89

Part II – Jacqueline's Influences

My Passion to Influence Becomes a Struggle & My Testimony

Chapter 11 – Starting Our Life Together / Family Drama 109

Chapter 12 – Breaking the Scheming Mindset 115

Chapter 13 – Our Separation 129

All Things Are Possible with God

Chapter 14 – My Walk with God 145

Closing Comments from a Loving Husband and a Loving Wife

A Letter from Dee 149

His Prayer 151

A Letter from Jacqueline 151

A Letter from Jaclyn 153

A Letter from Daijah 154

A Letter from Kamon 155

Appendix 157

Acknowledgements

To my wife who has inspired me to continue to push on during the times when I wanted to give up. I thank you immensely for continuing to be the driving force in my life.

To my little ladies Jaclyn & Daijah who continue to be my motivation and purpose in my attempt to leave a legacy for both of you, your children, and your children's children.

To my nephew Kamon, you have been instrumental in my desire to mentor and save our children from self-destruction and unwittingly encouraged me to guide our youth.

To my parents that have prayed fervently on my behalf. Thank you for your continued prayers, strength and belief in my abilities.

To my in-laws Mr. & Mrs. Johnson, thank you for the positive encouragement to continue to grow and lead my family keeping God as the center of our household.

To our editor Rhonda Green thank you for your hard work in making our thoughts comprehensible to the readers.

Prologue

I envisioned my body in a casket. My family, high-school classmates, and friends packed the old church. My skin was "black as soot" as the old people use to say. My once brown, caramel skin tone was now altered by the embalming fluid. I felt so terrible leaving this life behind; my parents, brothers, and friends looked to be taking it very hard. The pain caused a burning sensation in my chest. There was a lump in my throat from seeing my mother's tears, and the emotions would not allow any words to come out as I tried to comfort her. As I scanned the church, I heard whispers of people talking about the suicide "Why has he killed himself?"

"No!" I yelled. I awoke suddenly from my sleep. Tears ran down my face. I was covered in sweat. The hair on my arms stood straight up. "It's not fair; I'm too young to die!" Then I realized it was just another nightmare. I felt I was losing my mind. The signs had been there for months. I begged for help. I was slipping into a depression. I was in unfamiliar territory, struggling to distinguish reality from my nightmares. I had visions of the destruction of the world as we know it. I saw a world filled with death, violence, and nuclear war. All humanity was struggling to live each day. I saw a world of good versus evil, angels and demons, the apocalypse… a spiritual war. I felt trapped, alone, and afraid in a world that was very unfamiliar. As I interacted with family and friends, I felt I was treated as if I had the plague or three eyes. I felt abandoned by my family and friends. I prayed constantly, begging God to show me my purpose. I begged Him to take the stress away from me. I prayed that He would restore my mental competence. I prayed that He would give me a sign that He had plans for my life.

I grabbed my father's .32 revolver from his dresser drawer. The house was so quiet it was eerie. I reflected on my dream and felt an inexplicable peace. I felt guilty for leaving my family and friends behind, but my mind was at peace. I couldn't remember the last time I didn't have a nightmare. I couldn't tell you the last time I felt in control of my thoughts. As I stared at the gun in my hand, I weighed my options. Should I continue down the path of nightmares, loneliness, betrayal, and feeling out of place? Should I seek the tranquil energy and peace I remembered feeling during my dream? I asked myself, *how did I get here?* A young man who graduated high school, joined the military, and attended college was now looking down the barrel of a gun. *How is this God's plan?* I asked myself. *What does He want from me?*

"I want my life back!" I yelled at this invisible God. "Why would you allow this to happen to me? What cruel Father would do this to someone He loved?" I felt the anger boiling through my veins. I thought of the look of disgust I saw in the eyes of those who didn't understand what I was going through. I made one last final appeal to this God ... the God of my parents. I placed one bullet into the chamber of the revolver and spent the cylinder. I raised the gun to my head and with my eyes closed listened to my heart beat race. "Dear God, if you have any plans for my life ... please show me now. God, if you are real, do something supernatural; make your presence known to me in plain English. Father, give me a sign even an idiot can understand." I pulled the hammer back on the revolver and prayed for forgiveness.

Introduction

This book is about the life of Demetrius Irick, all the obstacles and trials he experienced. In this book, you will find a dysfunctional family riddled by alcoholism and lack of attention, which opened Demetrius up to a life of crime and bad choices. The reader will learn how this foundation created a void between siblings, pushed the family apart and fueled suicidal thoughts. As parents, you will learn signs that will enable you to detect the type of children your kids are hanging around. You will recognize the clear red flags and learn to pay closer attention to them. You will have an opportunity to establish better communication with your children, which can help minimize long-term problems and issues.

You will see how male chauvinist views encouraged promiscuous behavior in my life's story. You will learn the burden those views place on a young female who stands by a young man when she sees potential in him. Women, mothers, and daughters - please stick with your man if you have a good one. But be 100% sure there are signs that he not only can be what you need, but also that he has the desire and willingness to become what you expect. In this book, you will read about the struggles everyone faced to raise a Black Boy into a Black Man. This story is based on real life events. The characters, names, and some situations have been adapted to eliminate the use of actual persons' names.

The
Background Story

Chapter 1
The Early Years

The year was 1973, the beginning of the Internet and the year of *American Graffiti*, *The Exorcist*, Roe vs. Wade, and Watergate. Inflation was up by 6%. With so much going on in the country, I was resilient in my quest to be a part of this world. I grew up with the support and love of my parents, siblings, and grandparents. We were raised in modest means, having the necessities of life and little wants. I remember early in my childhood not having a lot: the welfare peanut butter that locked up your jaws, the long thick block of government cheese, powdered milk, and King Vitamin[1] cereal. These were some of our common choices. We sometimes had Kaboom[2] cereal, if we were lucky. I remember being sent to the nearest park or school to receive the free subsidy lunches every day during

---

[1] King Vitamin cereal is produced by Quaker Oats.

[2] Kaboom is a breakfast cereal produced by General Mills.

our summer breaks. The neighborhood kids would walk to the nearest park and swing on the monkey bars or throw rocks at each other. We played football and basketball and ran around exploring the area, which were our means of excitement.

Those were simpler times, the days when everyone in the neighborhood had the right to cut your behind if you were misbehaving. Those were the days when kids could be kids. There was little worry about the perverse minds of today's adults, the kidnapping, raping, child molesting, etc. Those were times when kids hated being in the house for anything. They would rather be outside doing something that kept them active and physical. The activities of today's kids, sitting around all day playing video games, would not cut it in those days. Those were the times of the corner store. There wasn't anything like a Wal-Mart or Target, but Kmart and Roses were the super centers or main hubs and connections to purchase household items. It was the time of penny gums, when five or ten cents could get you Now & Laters or Fortune Gum[3]. There was still subtle racism in Orangeburg. The white kids had their own high school, which was Orangeburg Prep, and the black kids went to Orangeburg Wilkinson. The racial divide was understood and tolerated in this small town, which was still so far behind the times. I remember going to the Five and Dime store in the heart of the city and wondering why the White people would move out of our way as if we had leprosy or why we never

---

[3] Popular gum that is now discontinued.

were able to play with their kids while in the stores. The stores had a lot of toys on display, and parents would let their kids find toys on the shelves to occupy their time while waiting in line, paying their phone bill, or whatever the adults were doing. I remember feeling puzzled when I looked into a young white child's eyes as I approached her to play. She backed away from me as if I had done something to her - as if she had seen a ghost and just started running. My mother grabbed our hands and with a look of anger, proceeded out of the store. I knew better than to get on my mother's nerves when she was upset, so my brother and I just sat silently in our seats and gazed out of the windows on our ride home.

My parents had a high school education, but our homework was a little challenging for them, so if I didn't take good notes I couldn't get re-enforcement at home. I would hear them brag to their friends about how smart I was and how well the teachers spoke of me. It truly made me feel loved and kept me motivated to continue my efforts. It also motivated me to be successful and understand my role in the family. I took the boasting as a sign of affection since it happened rarely. As kids, our days started with our parents waking us up around 6 a.m. We were rushed out of the house to walk to school so we could have breakfast there. While walking to school, kids find the darndest things to get into. As we walked, our crew grew. We collected other kids to walk as a pack. In my neighborhood alone, we started off with three kids, but once we hit the next block, grew to eight or sometimes fifteen kids. We chased the girls around and played chest–nut–feel. We threw rocks, eggs, and anything else at people and cars. We picked fights with each other, especially with someone who wasn't cool. One year, we picked a fight with a new student and actually broke his collarbone. I remember that everybody got in trouble for that act. The principal gave everyone detention and made them clean the cafeteria. I didn't get disciplined since I was the ringleader. Instead, she taught my friends not to be followers at any time. Conversely, I learned a valuable lesson, by getting all my friends in trouble; for example, to be careful of my actions and how they affect others. Decisions we make affect more than ourselves; we have to be very conscience of our actions.

Life was great, as I could remember. There was a lot of laughing and playing with my two brothers in the household. One Saturday morning, we were playing in the house with a little football. Stuart was the quarterback, as usual. We were in the middle of a down when Stuart all of a sudden stopped and said he had to go to the bathroom. Levar and I didn't know any better as we continued to play. Just as I threw the ball, my mother walked in the house and the ball hit the china closet. I heard my mom yell, "I know y'all not playing in this house!" Needless to say, we got our behinds cut that day, and Stuart acted as if he didn't know anything about it. I knew from that day that I've got to be like that; I have to know when trouble is coming my way and find a way to avoid it. I truly didn't want to have a lot of those days of getting my behind torn out of the frame. Stuart taught me a valuable lesson that day. As I grew, I learned how to avoid getting my behind cut. I found myself to be obedient and listened to what my parents said. I remembered that he would go on all kinds of trips away from home; that was exciting to me. I was just in middle school but it motivated me to follow his lead. I picked up the trumpet in fifth grade and began to explore my musical interest. I wasn't that great, but I was usually able to place myself within the top five chairs of the class in my group. I studied hard and practiced even harder with other friends from the neighborhood. Mr. Clark was my music teacher and a fellow trumpeter. I continued to play in the band until my sophomore year of high school. The discipline was important for me later in life. It allowed me to have a base to come back to after I experimented with the world and found myself lost in the streets. I went back to the essence of my being, which enabled me to rededicate myself and separate from the self-destruction in which I later found myself.

High school was okay for me but not at first. My freshman and sophomore years were the worst. I was a virgin, had dark spots all over my face, and had really bad acne. I was overweight, and all my friends called me Meatball. I quickly developed a complex and had self-esteem issues. I struggled with low self-esteem for many years, as these feelings were imposed on me at such an early, impressionable age. However, my big brother Stuart was again my saving grace during a trying time.

During my sophomore year of high school, Stuart asked my dad to cosign, and they bought me a motorcycle. It was the best present I could remember ever having! The joy of riding a motorcycle was very exhilarating. It's a kind of peace that only other cyclist would appreciate. I felt independent. I then began to focus on making sure my grades were up to par, plus I had a job to help me keep gas in the bike. I rode that bike everywhere, even during the winter months. My obsessive behavior led Grandpa Irick to store my bike in his shed during the winter months. With little to pass my time, I tried dating - with many failed efforts from the very beginning!

It seemed like any girl I had, my cousin Tray would always manage to take. First, there was Stephanie. Man, I had the craziest crush on her. I told the guys in my neighborhood about her, but I was so afraid to act on those feelings that I got stuck and did not make a move at all. I never came out and told Stephanie how much I wanted to be her boyfriend. I first met her in the summer of '86. Our mothers were part of the same organization, Eastern Stars[4]. We would go to a camp each summer, and I remember she looked like a model on television. At the tender age of 13, I was dazzled by her beauty. I was speechless in her presence. I told my brother to go tell her that I liked her, always pushing him to do my dirty work. I finally got an opportunity to speak with Stephanie once in high school, but by then she was way out my

---

[4] Fraternal organization for men and women.

league. My cousin had pushed up on her, and they were dating. I had such a love/hate relationship with my cousin, after years of telling him, how much I liked this girl, he dated her. It was psychologically hard for me to see them together. I was pissed off but always found a way to restrain myself from showing hurt or pain. It was so painful to see them together. I secretly despised Stephanie for not being able to see through my cousin. I felt he wasn't good enough for her. He didn't truly love her as I did. I allowed these emotions to get the best of me, and eventually, pent-up anger and aggression initiated my resentment towards females. However, I swallowed my feelings and put on the face as if nothing bothers me. I used denial as my mechanism to deal with pain. My cousin did this same thing to me with maybe two other girls whom I either dated or displayed some type of connection. I learned then that women could not be trusted. I began to view women differently after the pain I felt through these encounters, with my cousin spearheading my lesson. Tray often told me not to fall in love, just to spend time with the women, sex 'em and move on to the next one. This behavior was encouraged on many levels by our fathers and other male father figures in our lives. This behavior was subliminally and deliberately taught, as well as condoned. It was an unwritten rule that manhood was determined by the number of girls you could conquer or sleep with. This bred a lack of respect for my female counterparts and eventually I developed a complex in which I didn't trust any female. The things I despised of my father, I had become. I treated many women with no respect.

I remember getting high fives and confirmation when my brothers and I had many girls coming by the house. The more women we had, the more of a man we were considered to be. That was the mentality of my peers and the older men I was brought up around. The only love was the time you were in the bed; other than that, everything was about getting into the bedroom. I knew guys who spent more time gaming, learning, and listening to women just to get them in the bed. The things men would do to sleep with women were crazy. I knew guys who would wait weeks - even months to sleep with a woman, and after they did, they would find a way to break up with them. It was all a game; divide and conquer was the mentality. The man in some form was no better than an old yard dog that didn't have any loyalty to one mate. The male dogs would follow behind any female dog in heat, and this is what I became: a dog, an old yard dog, afraid to commit to anyone out of fear of rejection, pain, and hurt.

The Beginning of the End

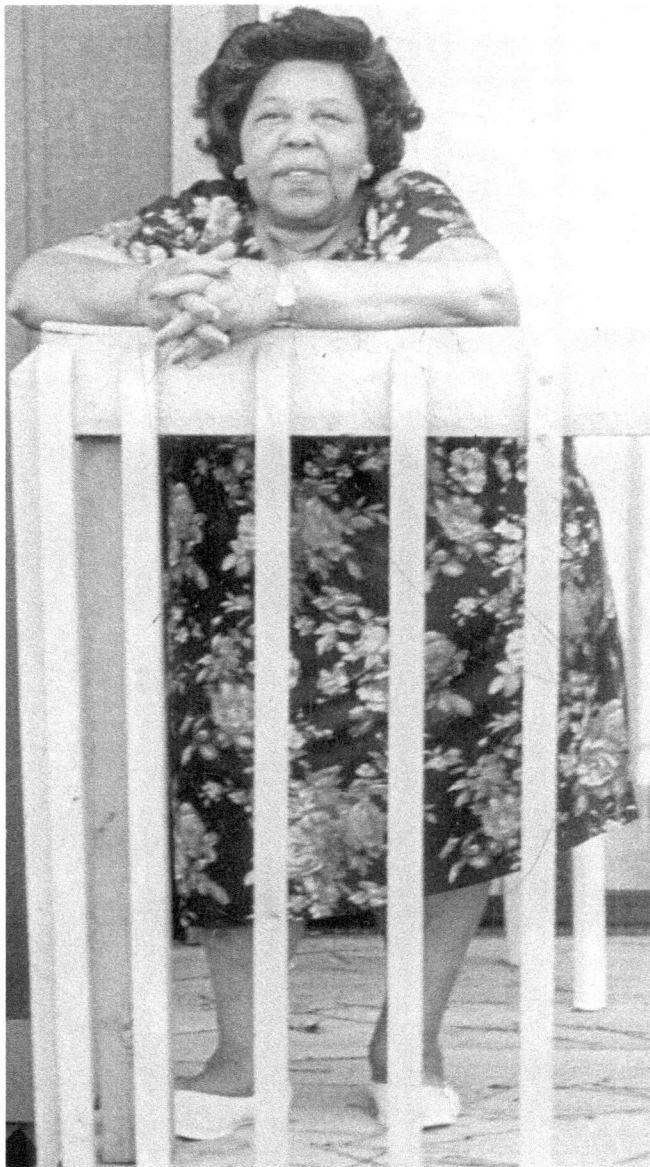

Chapter 2

The Background of Self-Destruction

Thomas Lee Irick son of Elden "Buck" Irick and Vertell "Sinky" Randolph was born in Calhoun County in June 1946. Sara Mae Pringle Irick, the daughter of Sarah Govan Pringle and Westley Pringle, produced three boys: Stuart, Demetrius, and Levar. I have two other siblings, a brother and sister, Calvin and Diane, born prior to my mother's union to my father. Born of modest means, my parents learned through hard work and sacrifice the true meaning of survival. They watched as their fathers and grandparents picked cotton in the hot South Carolina day. Times like these allowed both of my parents to learn to respect their parents' efforts as they sacrificed to put food on the table. Those lessons were used as my parents grew and decided to raise their own family.

Grandpa West, my mother's father, planted all types of vegetables - corn, collard greens, string beans and sugar cane. As I grew older, I reflected on his life examples. I learned hard work was okay. I also learned that choices have to be made, which sometimes requires a man to be out of the presence of his loved ones. It takes a lot of time, cultivating a garden. It takes commitment, dedication, and determination to watch and nurture a seed to grow and be fruitful. All of this takes time away from being in the house raising children or spending time with a wife. I understand that my grandfather made decisions to ensure his family had the necessities of life, and it required him to spend time away from the house. Even in today's world, most working adults spend more time at their jobs than at home. We have to find a healthy balance between work and home, but I know if a person doesn't work, he will not have anything in this life.

Grandma Pringle was the anchor of the Pringle family. She was the nucleus and the heartbeat of the family celebrations around the holidays. Yearly events gave us an opportunity to meet and interact with family members we very rarely had the opportunity to see or meet. Grandma Pringle would spend hours in the kitchen preparing our Thanksgiving or Christmas dinners. My grandmother's birthday was also on Christmas Day, which gave us a reason for huge celebrations on this day. The genuine closeness with Grandma Pringle wasn't there in comparison with the bond I had with my fathers' parents. It was as if the grandchildren were to be seen and not heard; therefore, as children we didn't get a lot of attention. I felt attentiveness was given more to bond with her children, as opposed to establishing a relationship with the grandkids. I learned not to alienate loved ones, as you never know who you may need in this life.

Grandma Irick was my heart and the bond we shared was unbreakable. I remember as a child in the '80s, my grandmother cleaned rich white peoples' houses as a means of extra income for the holidays. I never understood my grandmother's mentality – not to be self-sufficient. I noticed at an early age that she didn't have any true skills, or work traits to make her self-reliant. My grandmother's philosophy was that as long as the man took care of the house and bills, he was able to "be a man". She depended on my grandfather as a means of obtaining her necessities. My grandmother never got a driver's license; therefore, my grandfather took her everywhere she needed to go. Instead of following the women's movement for equal rights in the 1960s and 1970s, Grandma focused her time and efforts on being a good mother, grandmother, and wife, which she did very well. The stereotype of women in the early days was to be bearers of children and to keep the house clean. Grandma always opened her heart and home to everyone. There were no strangers with my grandma, and she never made anyone feel uncomfortable in her presence. The family was most important to her. I spent much of my time with her from an early age up until her dying day. Although grandma lacked her own sense of independence, I recall her telling me, "If they can do it, you can do it". This slogan was ingrained in my mind, and any time I was faced with a difficult situation, I thought of her and that quote. I learned the love of children from my grandmother. She always showed her affection to all children. As a child, I hated to get kisses from my grandmother; most kids didn't like this, especially as they grew older. But, my grandmother made it a ritual that every time she saw me, she'd shower me with "I love you" and kisses. After, my grandmother's death, I appreciated these memorable moments. Grandma also taught me perseverance and self-esteem. She always preached to me that I am just as good as or better than anyone else in this world. She told me that I am my own worst enemy and that I need to push myself past my own comfort level. Whatever I set my mind to, I can accomplish. The statement, "If they can do it, you can do it" alludes to the fact that we should never say what can't be accomplished, especially after someone else has already accomplished the same feat. We are all made in God's image and have the elements needed to be successful in our endeavors.

Grandpa Irick was the provider, the hustler, and a friend to many. His strong work ethic set the tone of fatherhood in the Irick family. With no formal schooling, he was forced to live a life of manual and physical labor, working sun up to sun down in the fields. My grandfather took those traits and used them to be a great provider for his family. After hours and on the weekends, Buck was a hustler, selling alcohol and running a "juke joint" from his own back yard. Every Friday night and some Saturday nights, Buck Irick's house was the place to be. People from all over the area would come by and drink, barbecue, cook out, and party until the early hours of the morning.

With this hustle mentality, money and popularity came envy, women, and a marriage in despair. From my grandfather, I learned some positive traits like it is okay to have multiple streams of income. My grandfather had different means of securing enough income to provide for his family. Grandpa Buck also enforced the need to have a strong work ethic. There were plenty of days I cleaned the hog and chicken pens or fed the livestock in order to earn a few dollars to spend in the stores. This taught me that nothing is free and that we need to work for everything we want.

I gained a strong work ethic from the males in my family and those in my bloodline. I also found this common denominator in all of the men in my family. Every single male required time away from his family. I once found it strange but have come to relish quiet time alone. I notice that I have developed some similar patterns. I enjoy my alone time which gives me a chance to think, and process my life. I also utilized this time to consider the direction I need to lead my family and the corrections I need to make to get them there. My wife couldn't understand why I was withdrawn and didn't want to spend time talking with her. She didn't understand why I was being rude. I also did not have very good communication skills. I kept everything bottled up inside of me. When I did speak, it was always out of frustration. I realized there was a connection between my grandparent's lack of communication skills and how it was unintentionally passed down throughout the males within the family as all the males struggled in this area in their relationships.

I also observed behaviors that fostered or encouraged extramarital affairs. The males encouraged promiscuity as a rite of passage, a way of defining all males and manhood. These celebrations, acknowledgements and encouragements, shaped my philosophy on women and relationships. I eventually followed the examples of the men around me. I adopted the philosophy that it was okay to have sexual relationships with multiple women and that it was the thing that men do. Women and men were different, and this was a man's need. Sexual encounters were an act of physical fulfillment, not an expression of feelings. These ideas later posed a major problem for me as I grew to analyze my view of relationships and marriage.

My father was surrounded by this behavior; it laid the same foundation for his viewpoint on women and the definition of their roles in the household. The subliminal messages his father, and his mother sent condoning these behaviors led to a cycle yet to be broken. This chauvinistic manner didn't sit right with my mother, and it caused a lot of hurt and pain in their marriage for years to come. But, in an everchanging world, some of his ideas were outdated and stretched the marriage in a proportion that hurt its growth for a time. The mindset had to shift if the marriage were to be healthy. My parents struggled with several issues throughout their marriage. Early in the marriage it was money and infidelity, and then later children weighed heavily on the marriage. This pushed them apart in several ways. My father in the beginning wasn't big on going to church, but my mom was insistent and made sure all the children were actively involved in the church at an early age. My father spent his weekends drinking with his friends, usually at his parents' house or the local bars and nightclubs. This divide along with the absence of our father brought my siblings and I closer to our mother and Grandma Irick.

In essence, my parents lived totally separate yet resided under the same roof. I only recall my parents taking us on one family vacation, to Disney World in the late 1980's and man, it was the only fond memory of my life as a child. The vacation marked a time in my life when we seemed connected. As I look back, my father was proud of his ability to afford to take us. My mother, my siblings and I were excited, and it felt good to share this time together, interacting as a family.

Sara Mae Pringle Irick was the baby girl born of the union of Sarah Pringle and Westley Pringle. She was a single teenage mom with two children. Sara was married by age 18, and her mother raised the two children she had conceived out of wedlock. Her eldest children were known to us as Calvin and Diane. For my little brother and me, having other siblings who were our eldest brother and sister but who were only referred to by name was confusing. We never celebrated meaningful days and times together outside of Thanksgiving and Christmas. We didn't acknowledge our siblings birthdays or attend each other's graduations, recitals, etc. An extension of our family lived only 10 minutes away, yet we were so far apart. As I grew, I found this to be characteristic of a dysfunctional family life. I grasp to understand the relationship; it just never made really good sense to me. I recall my father referring to Diane's children as Sara's grandchildren. I never understood the reasoning behind the divide, but this has created what seems like an unreachable distance today. Although we all get together during the holidays and for barbecues, there is little connection between the extended families. We are relatives getting together out of tradition, versus relatives interacting from a true bond. However, I finally saw some changes in my father's mindset about his children. I recently heard my father make reference to Calvin and Diane, and he included them in his count of children. It was the first time I ever heard him make this type of reference. I truly believe that time brings changes, and the fact that people can change is the key to development and growth. We all have the unique opportunity to change our current situation and state of mind, but we have to be willing, to be open to others' points of view and have the desire to do the right thing.

I felt closer to my mother than my two brothers did. No one could speak about or mistreat Mama. My mother was the disciplinarian of our house. She was more temperamental and adamant about making sure we did the right things, as opposed to my dad taking the more modest approach. My mother worked from 8 a.m. to 4 p.m., Monday through Friday. I remember always having a hot meal growing up. We only ate out on Friday nights and occasionally on Saturday. There was a dish assigned for every day of the week. Every Sunday after church, we gathered at the table for dinner. Our

Sunday dinners seemed to bring our family together. This was the only time during the week that we all sat together at the table. However, there was minimal to no conversation at the table. Sunday dinner could have been our focal point for connecting and communicating. Looking over my life today, I realize there were things I did not understand but did not dare question. For example, why did my mother allow or tolerate the lack of respect for females? Why didn't she make it a mandate that all her boys respect every girlfriend or females in general? Especially after she fought so hard to earn my father's respect and tried to teach him to be a better father figure. Nonetheless, my mom's discipline kept me at bay and away from trouble in my adolescent years. It reminded me that I had to limit things I should get involved in. My mother's acceptance of the derogatory behaviors displayed toward women confirmed that it was okay to be disrespectful toward females. I don't remember ever being scorned by my mother for dating multiple women while I was growing up, so I felt it was okay. This was life in the Irick house, which did not seem strange to me until I began building a family and a life of my own. My wife Jacqueline and kids Jaclyn and Daijah came along years later, but the divide and dysfunction of my childhood household created a cycle that I had to break. My motivation was my own family. We have vowed, Jacqueline and I, to establish such a family. Each day we work hard at that goal.

I was born the middle child of Thomas Lee Irick and Sara Irick. This union produced three boys: Stuart (the eldest), myself, and Levar (the youngest). I came into this world on July 29, 1973, around 1:49 p.m., at the Orangeburg Regional Medical Center. Weighing in at 4 pounds, 13 ounces, I was a preemie struggling to "breathe." As I reflect back on my life, I realize I was born fighting to live to be a part of this world. The odds have been stacked against me, but still I rise[1]. I also see that God has been fighting for me, as well. My mom drove herself to the hospital because my father was not around during this time. My father's priorities weren't always right during those days. My father's pastime was drinking and cooling with his friends. He was an "absentee" father. The term absentee was used because he was physically in the house, but his presence wasn't a positive influence in the lives of his children. My father didn't spend time going over homework, reading books to the children, or encouraging us to excel in school. My father disciplined us when necessary, and if we were totally out of line. At the time, my father wasn't leading by example or showing any affection that kids desire and need. I vowed never to be this way if I decided to have children and become a father. The popular hangout during this time was a convenience store during the day and a hole-in-the-wall club at night right down the street from our home. The locals would get together for a night of drugs, alcohol, sex, and pool, with the jukebox playing that year's favorite hits. This was an every week thing for my daddy.

In addition to one's upbringing, there is at least one historical event in everyone's lifetime that molded your

---

[1] Still I Rise is a famous poem by Dr. Maya Angelou.

view of the world. Orangeburg, SC was marred by an event that is now called The Orangeburg Massacre. Although a lot of Blacks didn't discuss it openly, there was an underlying tension and division among racial lines. Even in the '80s, there were subtle racial lines drawn, and at times, racial tension would show its ugly head. Although the city was integrated, it was still very much segregated. Rarely did blacks and whites intermingle outside of the necessary requirements of work, hospital, police intervention, public service activities, etc. February 8, 1968, was a dark day for Orangeburg and its citizens. Students from South Carolina State University (SCSU), formerly South Carolina State, tried to bowl in the only bowling alley in the city. The owners were true "rednecks" and refused to allow black students to bowl in their establishment. The tension grew quickly, and the racial lines were divided. Violence erupted. Police were dispatched to control the crowd. During the process police clubbed several female students. At the end of the day, 28 students were injured, and three were dead.

Hundreds of students began to riot. After a couple of days of escalating tension, state troopers were called to enforce crowd control. The white troopers were eager to display their superiority. One of the students threw a banister rail into the crowd, striking a trooper. An officer whose gun was filled with buckshot pellets opened fire; his lead was followed by all the officers. As they fired into the crowd students were shot in the back as they ran for cover. Many were trampled as everyone tried to get away. Of the 66 troopers at the scene, eight later told FBI agents that they had fired their riot guns at the students after hearing shots. Some fired more than once. A ninth patrolman said he fired his .38 caliber Colt service revolver six times as "a spontaneous reaction to the situation". At least one city policeman - who later became police chief - fired a shotgun. This tragic episode had a lasting psychological effect on the people and the city. This is the Orangeburg I remember as a child.

Chapter 3

The Dark Side

The time that I first changed from being a nice guy was when I asked my parents to let me go to a dance. I was a good child, so they didn't have any reason not to allow me to go to the Upward Bound dance. I remember the day as if it were yesterday. We were walking to the party, which was always held at Claflin College, one of the local colleges in Orangeburg. My friends and I spent two hours drinking Seagram's Gin, Vodka, and Peppermint Gin chased with Old English, Mickey, Crazy Horse, and Red Bull. We were determined to be out of our minds by the time we got to this party. Needless to say, by the time we arrived, I was juiced up way past anyone's limits. I was with my crew and ready to have fun as we were in route to the dance. As we entered the event, all I could think about was violence. I felt as if I were invincible and that no one could stop me. I walked around the crowded gym with my chest out, practically begging someone to give me any reason to unleash the demons the alcohol had stirred up inside of me. The alcohol seemed to awaken a sleeping giant. I felt a sense of arrogance I'd never known. I felt the excitement I wasn't accustomed to experiencing. My blood was racing, heart pounding, as I scanned the gym looking for trouble. Near the end of the party, I got my wish. Some poor dude bumped into me, and I beat this guy until he could not move. My crew stomped and kicked, as we showed this guy who we were. Each punch I threw landed on his face, with a concentration of left eye, right eye. I was determined to make him look into the mirror the next morning and remember who had given him the souvenir. I was rushed outside by my crew to avoid detection from the authorities. Once outside the event, we ran until we were back on Campus Drive. When we were back in our environment, we candidly discussed our beat down. We celebrated the victory as each of us recounted our memories of what part we had played. That single night began the change in my life. I remember feeling invincible after the fight, feeling exhilarated and full of energy. The next day when I woke up and reflected on my exploits, I felt no remorse for my actions. I felt I was living a double life. I felt I was living out a fantasy like Clark Kent realizing his capabilities. It's hard to go back into the shadow after getting a glimpse of the spotlight. It felt so good—better than the ordinary role I had become used to. The quiet, laid-back, reserved person I was as a child was tainted and I worried briefly if I would ever turn back into that person.

The very next week was the same thing. We drank past any comprehension and found someone on whom to release our frustrations. This pattern continued week after week. We carried this energy wherever we went together. Sometimes it spilled over at the local restaurant. McDonalds was one of the popular locations after football games and dances. I remember picking on some couple who was coming out of the restaurant. They were dressed in a tuxedo and gown, which made me believe they were headed to a prom or dance. I commented on his girl's dress—well her behind. I must admit my behavior was inappropriate. The guy in return made a reference about my mother. Well, I was on top of this guy before he realized what hit him. I remember hearing his girl rush to his side, as she screamed for me to stop hitting him. I looked right through her as I continued to mop the ground with his tuxedo. We went at it as I stomped him until the cops came, then I bolted. The poor old cop tried to give chase but was unable to keep up with the speed and agility of a young teenager. The excitement of my actions and acceptance of my peers and others psychologically added fuel to my fire. I never reflected on my actions, never took the time to think about how I changed my victims' lives, or how they felt. I was driven solely by my emotion and sense of worth. I felt that I had moved out of the shadows of the guys who I associated with.

Most of my crew had talents that I didn't possess, and I had to compensate in other areas. Big Money had the gift of gab and could charm the pants off any girl. Elva resembled Big Daddy Kane and females were fascinated by his looks. All my other friends were thugs and hustlers and had money to buy things a kid my age desired. So, unequipped with physical good looks or the ability to speak well, I turned to the thuggish route for notoriety.

The next week, back at the weekly party, Elva was about to get into a fight with an old boyfriend of a girl he was dating. The ex-boyfriend was an upper classmen and a football player. This guy was well known around the school. Of course, the young man didn't like Elva because of this, but he approached us during the event and threatened not only Elva, but me as well. I didn't take this well, and I wasn't going to swallow it. I told Elva that I was going to knock this guy out. Elva, the cool-headed one, advised me not to, but my eyes were set on the disrespect. It would not be tolerated. At that point in time, a switch flipped on in my head that made me determined to knock this kat out. This was during the time when Mike Tyson ruled over the boxing world, and I felt I was Tyson that night. I circled around the party, awaiting the best time to make my move. The guy was surrounded by his football buddies, and there wasn't any way for me to get to him. After surveying him for about what seemed to be an hour, I decided he was going down regardless. I don't remember when I lost Elva in the midst of all of this, but I remember walking toward the guy with pure hatred. I walked through his entire circle of friends. He had his back turned to me. I tapped him on the shoulder and, as he turned toward me, hit him with the force of 10 bricks to his dome. It was as if he fell down in slow motion. Everything was in slow motion. I noticed his friends looking on in disbelief, some scrambling to his aid, others looking for me. I remember the crowd's faces, some horrified, and some laughing. As the crowd rushed around to see who and what had transpired, I got lost in the crowd. My adrenaline was going faster than I could imagine. I felt as if I were King Kong that night, and that helped to send me to a platform with friends I thought I would never meet. I remember that people who had never known my name or dared speak to me in the past now knew who I was. I remember meeting the bad boys or the "Hill" crew - the kids who were hustlers, truly living the life of the hustler with the thug mentality I was beginning to display. After that night, I started hanging with a different element of kids. I was now hanging with the bad boys of the town, and my name rang bells in some circles. An ordinarily quiet student, I was going down the path of destruction. I liked the feeling of being recognized by the people. I liked that people knew my name. People would recount the stories they heard about my exploits. There was such joy and enthusiasm in their voices as they relived the events. I was headed toward my destruction and downfall, but I only saw it as a new beginning to a world that would never forget my name. The behaviors, fights and destruction became fun ways to express ourselves. The ability to live outside of the norm was my motivation to continue on the path. Fueled with peer pressure and the desire to please, I continued my exploits, and the gamble and risks I took increased.

As this behavior continued, after each party I would look for someone to brawl with. I remember asking the crowd arrogantly who they wanted me to knock out tonight. The first person they pointed to got it - simple as that. It felt so good to finally be recognized. After years of being a nice guy, passed over by girls and having only a small circle of true friends, I now was being recognized on a whole different level.

Growing up, I always felt I didn't have the support or even the options to live a better life, coming out of Orangeburg or "OB" as the locals called it. I felt that it was such a cesspool that bred ignorance and fostered an environment of violence, drugs, and high murder rates. There wasn't anything for a young African American to do in this city, which opened the door for energetic kids to get involved in gangs, drugs, sex, and illicit activities as a means of excitement. This kept the kids from thinking about all the things they didn't have in this life. The vast majority of the children in my neighborhood or in surrounding areas participated in the selling of drugs. The "Hill" was a thriving block where the hustlers, drug pushers, addicts, and girls meet and make money. It was a poorly developed neighborhood of row houses, mobile homes, abandoned houses and stores. The neighborhood was riddled with middle and high school dropouts, drug addicts and dealers of all ages. It was known to have the best dope in town, and the dealers were aggressively trying to market their product. The Hill was well known as the hustle spot in OB. Its reputation was known not only in Orangeburg but in neighboring counties like Denmark, Bamberg, Bowman, Charleston, and Columbia. After a major initiative to crackdown on drugs in the '80s, the Hill was shut down, and the drugs relocated to the Campus Drive area, Stilton Road, Sprinkle Avenue, and the Edisto Drive area. It's amazing how the local sheriff spoke boldly about how they were able to eliminate the drugs and now the neighborhood was safe. He spoke about how they were successful in eliminating the drugs and the infamous "Hill," but he never spoke about everyone just moving less than a mile away to set up shop. Same people different place. Although my parents tried to keep me from becoming a product of my environment, the glitter, excitement, and fast life caught my eyes and attention. I started meeting kats in the drug game, and as my mom use to say association brings assimilation.

Now I went to parties at the Foxy 44 Lounge, and I had a name. I was being noticed by girls who had never given me the time of day. I had problems with girls in the past because my shyness didn't allow me to speak to many females. If I hadn't been placed in a position where we had to speak to each other, I probably wouldn't speak to the females; that's how nervous they made me. But now women approached me, and I relished this newfound celebrity spotlight. My crew would always find girls, and now I finally got my chance, and it felt good. It finally felt good to have someone interested in me. Just the previous year, I had been in the band, trying to be a good schoolboy. It's amazing how bad news travels quickly. People would talk about what they heard. "Did you hear Demetrius was in a fight?" I was at a club and was approached by a young lady who asked me to dance. I followed her onto the dance floor and began to get my two-step on. In the midst of our dancing, she told me how she had heard about the fights I had won and how she loved to be with a winner.

I began hustling, selling drugs here and there, and experimenting with drugs, mostly cocaine. I stayed out all times of the night, including school nights, sometimes drinking in my back yard until midnight. My life became a cycle of sex, drugs, and violence. I realized that as I continued in this lifestyle, I found myself to be bolder in my exploits and attitude. Taking chances became the norm. I was drinking and driving daily. Some days, my crew and I rode around getting drunk and snorting cocaine. We pulled into a McDonald's drive thru, and a bee flew into the passenger's window as I pulled up to the window. It landed on the windshield, and Dave, in his drunken state, smacked the bee with his hand and cracked the windshield. We were all like, *My God!* We thought I was never going to be able to drive my father's car again. We devised a plan to burglarize all the neighboring cars as a result of our misdeed. The next morning as I lay in my bed, I heard my father and several of the neighbors discussing their vehicles and trying to determine what crazy kids might have done such a thing and why.

It was no longer cool to be the first person in class. I entered class after the bell rang and found the seat closest to the back of the class. The monotony of school became boring as opposed to the level of energy and excitement from the nightlife. I found myself in a different place spiritually. I tried to remain the person my parents had raised, but I was slowly turning into what the nightlife was creating. I was getting farther and farther away from the innocent child my parents knew. I was becoming so distant from my parents. I couldn't relate to them any longer. I felt they were so disconnected from reality, my reality, that I didn't have time to teach them or bring them up to speed; therefore, they were excluded from the transformation I was going through.

It became too much for me to cover as I stopped doing my homework because I'd rather go outside and find something else to get into. I'd rather hang with the cool guys, drinking during the day and smoking cigarettes, selling drugs, snorting cocaine or smoking weed. I began to be introduced to other kids who were legends in the street life. The kids were hustlers, killers, and moneymakers in the drug game. I began to see kids my age making thousands of dollars a day selling drugs. I was now exposed to the dark world. I couldn't believe that my parents had kept me sheltered. I was in a place I never knew existed prior to my exploits. My spirit was in darkness, and I acted out all the exploits the dark world introduced to me. I became comfortable in the darkness. My philosophy on life became bleak. My choice of music was different, too. I enjoyed the music that was derogatory toward women, calling them bitches and hoes. I liked songs that spoke of violence. I could rap any truly hardcore lyrics, as I had committed them to memory. I only wanted to watch mob movies or something that had to do with sex, drugs, and violence.

These were just some of the many examples of the thuggish mind. It was the beginning of the deterioration of my morals and values. The change was so subtle that I didn't even realize it had happened until years later. We would travel to neighboring schools and towns to date the girls and cause havoc to the local guys. We created rivalries and caused tension between the neighboring counties. This behavior continued throughout my high school years, but it began to diminish after I graduated.

Chapter 4

The Escape From O.B.

After high school, I knew I needed to get away from the area. My feeble attempt to leave started with my joining the military at my cousin's request. I looked up to my cousin, because everything always came so easily to him. He had the life I wanted to live. I thought he made a lot of sense when explaining the benefits he reaped in joining. Several weeks later, I joined and left home for the first time to explore the world outside of the small town I lived in. I finally got a chance to learn how much more was out there and what life had to offer after leaving Orangeburg.

I was sent to Fort Knox, Kentucky for basic training in September 1991. That was a scary flight, as the entire previous night I had been out all night snorting cocaine. My heart felt as if it were about to come out of my chest. I snorted right up to the minute of checking into the MEPS (Military Entrance Processing Station). While in the building, you are given a physical, assigned a job, and sworn into the military. I was on the airplane high as a kite. I had the burning craving for a cigarette, and I couldn't smoke anymore after joining because of the physical conditioning needed.

Again, my state of mind didn't change because I left Orangeburg. I quickly collaborated with a guy from upstate New Jersey. We seemed to hit if off quickly; both of us had attitude problems. Jones was always getting in trouble with our commanders. I found myself drawn to this behavior, and we became cool. Eventually, he was my sidekick. Needless to say, in Kentucky, I found a way to go to the PX and get a pack of cigarettes. Even worse, I jogged briskly through the woods to get a smoke; over a mile from our military base. I lit cigarettes back to back, in hopes of achieving a high before realizing half the pack was gone.

While in the military, I finally learned discipline. It was subtle, and I fought it tooth and nail. However, when I reflected at the end of the training, I realized it was well worth it and that I needed it. I was able to take orders from a male figure, which I didn't do very well from my father. After being transferred to Fort Jackson in South Carolina, I realized that I was able to follow the orders of my superiors without any emotional desire to rebel. I continued to see beyond my small town mindset. I realized there was so much more out there in the world that I could be a part of. Outside of my attitude problem and disdain for authority, I had begun to see a small change in myself. I realized if left to my own devices, I could generally do the right thing. I decided that I would enroll in college and try to change my circle of friends.

My freshman year in college was similar to my freshman year in high school, and I didn't like that road. I felt uncomfortable in class. I was nobody again. No one knew me in most of my classes. Every blue moon, I saw a familiar face on campus. I began to feel insecure again. I felt like a nerd and out of my element. I occasionally ran into my old crew, and I missed them. I started heavily smoking weed every day, and the next thing I knew, I was cutting class. I missed the excitement and crazy things I did with the wolf pack. It's hard to describe the feeling of worthlessness that overcame me as I reflected on my feelings of isolation in class. I lost the desire to be different from everyone else. I wanted to fit in, to be accepted once again. I searched and longed for a bond with a female; I was looking for a female to fill a void in my heart, mind, and soul. I had a desire to feel connected to others. Before I could blink my eyes, I was a college drop out.

Why? I asked myself this question: Why are you hanging with these guys? My father advised me to stop hanging with some of the kids I was with. He said that when times get rough, you will realize who your true friends are, and they are not the current crew you hang out with. He said when trouble comes to find you; your so-called friends will not be anywhere to be found. My father's words came to pass several times before I finally learned the value of what he was trying so hard to teach me. I eventually succumbed to that desire and found myself right back in the same environment doing carjacking, trafficking guns and drugs, selling and doing drugs. I fell right back into Satan's trap.

Chapter 5

My Addiction

My first experience with cocaine was with Vince and Brian, smoking in front of Roscoe's. Roscoe's was part of a convenience store by day and a hang-out spot by night. At night, the life of prostitution and drugs came alive. Seeing this activity on a regular basis at a convenience store, from neighborhood friends and in everyday surroundings, appeared to be the thing to do. I wanted to be with the "in crowd," so I started smoking Newport. The first time I smoked, I thought the cigarettes smelled like cherries. They *were* "cherries," or as I was told, cigarettes laced with cocaine. At only 15, I was drinking Red Bull beer and getting high from cocaine. I occasionally smoked laced cigarettes when I ran into Dave, Vince, and Brian. It made me feel like I had an out-of-body experience, as if my spirit had left my body and I was now envisioning myself from a distance. I experienced an overwhelming desire for violence. I felt that I could live the life I saw on TV and in music videos. I remember thinking I could kill an army. Under the influence of cocaine, I became belligerent, a stark difference from my attitude outside of the drugs. No one could do me any harm.

I used to sneak out of my bedroom window and escape into the nightlife right at the end of my block. The hustlers and hoes were all a two-minute walk away. It was normal for me to wake up and smoke a joint like people smoked cigarettes. Within a year of smoking cherries, I upgraded to snorting cocaine two to four times a month for nearly seven years of my life. In addition to alcohol and drugs, I smoked weed daily. I smoked cigarettes and black and mild cigars for more than 15 years and drank alcohol from age 15 to 36. I finally, through the grace of God, have been able to put down the alcohol, drugs, and other addictions. My addictions cost me so much that I truly didn't understand the enormity of all that I lost or could have had if I had been a clear-thinking individual. I could have reached so many souls and given them a better example to follow. I could have spent time with my family to make our relationships stronger and better. I could have been a role model to my younger brother as a straight A student and a disciplined child. Instead, I lived a life of drugs, violence, and fornication. As a result, I lost my mental capability to produce a positive influence in my circle of friends. We are the sum of our decisions in this life.

Although I didn't always use cocaine on a daily basis, I was still an addict. I spent my entire paycheck on cocaine and partying whenever I decided to get high. I usually took off when I got paid and spent the weekend in sleazy hotels with women and drugs. There were times I would see my dealer four or five times in a day during those episodes. My day would start normally; I didn't like to get high in the middle of the day. Therefore, I conducted business as usual, cleaned the house, and completed the required chores my parents had for me. If I had to work, I went to work. It wasn't until it was dark that I searched out the drug dealers. I would rent out cheap hotel rooms to do drugs. I would spend all night chopping up the cocaine on a mirror with a razor blade and straw to snort. I always wrapped my cocaine inside of a dollar bill and folded it in the little pocket of my jeans. This enabled me to take the drugs in all clubs or any place I wanted to go. This went on for hours at a time, until I ran out or got low enough to make me want to go and get more. If my parents had any idea I was on drugs, they never intervened. I do recall my father making a comment that my "lips were black due to smoking," and my weight loss was obvious.

Parents, these are all red flags: weight-loss, black lips, dark fingernails, a change in attitude and mood swings. I became rebellious and easily confrontational. My dad's subtle comments, if backed by a strict intervention plan, may have pushed me in the right direction. We can't sit around idly when we see a problem; it's just not the best approach as a parent. This is not a stab at my father; I feel he really didn't know what to do and, through his indecisiveness, did nothing. We, as parents, have to lead our children, especially when we see them headed down the wrong path. If we see clear signs that there may be problems, we have to interject ourselves more into their lives and find the true nature of the problem. We have to question them, their friends, their teachers, and their behaviors—get professionals involved if needed. The last thing we want to do as parents is *nothing*! We can't sit back and just pray. We have to act on those prayers. Prayers and actions are the combination that will result in a change.

Hell on Wheels

Chapter 6

My Transition Period

I started having regular nightmares in May 1994. Since I could not recall the last time I had a bad dream, this shit really freaked me the heck out, especially the dreams of me dying. I would have dreams of my death in many forms. It was as if I saw death - my own death. I saw the people who loved me asking why. The dreams were so real they scared me into praying. There was a dream where I was struck by lightning, then I was in a car accident, I was shot, and dying of AIDS, to name a few. There was a dream that the whole world was going to be destroyed by a world war. There were nuclear attacks and the whole planet as we knew it was destroyed. The nuclear attacks killed billions of people, and only a few people survived. Some people and homes were underground; some were in military installations that were equipped just enough to protect them in these types of circumstances. Then, I started having dreams about going to jail and having to fight for my life. These dreams were detailed enough to remember when I awoke. The one dream that still horrifies me is the death of my grandmother, because this one came true. I dreamed my grandmother would die in her sleep and would die in my place. It was almost as if she sacrificed her life so that I could live mine. This dream was so crystal clear; it was alarming and scary at the same time. What was even odder was that my grandmother visited my house early one morning around 5 a.m. before sunup. She walked to my house, which was a job by itself. My grandmother was a very heavy woman, and the mere fact that she was out at that time in the morning and the look of terror on her face told me that something wasn't right. My parents brushed it off as if it were nothing, but my grandmother grabbed me. She put her arms around me to ensure she wasn't dreaming. She looked me in my eyes with such intensity that it reached my soul. She told me that she saw me in a dream and that I was dead. She walked all the way to my house praying and hoping it was a bad dream. She wanted to touch me to make sure I was alive and again that she wasn't dreaming. I realized at that moment that I knew so little about God and His divine interventions. Grandma told me that whatever I was involved in, associated with, or doing, that I needed to stop. She said she saw my death and that it was crystal clear that I wasn't living my life in the right manner. She pleaded that I change my ways and made me promise to stop what I was doing. Before she left, she mentioned that God doesn't reveal things for any reason. Less than

90 days later, my grandmother died. I reflected on that conversation with my grandmother when she had walked to my house early that morning to check on me. I gave up drugs at that moment but not all my bad habits.

I didn't read too much into it at first, thinking maybe grandma was just overreacting, so I continued my past deeds. However, upon hearing of my grandmother's death, that conversation came back to me. I thought back to the visions I had on a regular basis. I reflected on seeing my grandmother in a casket, and I blamed myself for it. It was such a terrible and painful situation for me. I temporarily lost my sanity. I held myself accountable for her death in many ways. After my grandmother died, I still had these nightmares, but the dreams somewhat shifted. I would dream about good and evil, God and the Devil, Hell and Heaven. I would have dreams of ghosts or entities trapped and forced to walk eternally throughout the earth with no sense of direction. I would think of the society in which we live today, and of all the evils in it. It seemed that my life was taking a turn for the worse. I knew by the dreams and experiences that it was time. It was time for me to turn my life around, and all these startling events I thought I saw or experienced were signs for me to find my way back, to myself and Jesus. I needed to find out why God created me. Thus, I hit the Bible searching for answers to my crazy thoughts. I searched for answers to the mystery of life and death. This was the first time I'd ever picked up a Bible to read it. The King James Version with the "Thee" and "Thou" was very hard for me to understand. I searched for the God of the universe to have a relationship with Him. I desired to be a better man, son, and friend to others; a better human being. I remember I would ask my parents questions about the Bible, but they were unable to answer my questions. I wondered why my parents couldn't answer these questions, since they went to church on a regular basis for as long as I could remember. I became discouraged by my parents and my new found attempt at faith. I was flustered by the inability to have a better understanding of our Creator. I trusted my parents to teach me the things I needed to be successful in life, and when I went to them with a genuine need and desire to be better and to have a better relationship with God, they couldn't help me, so I gave up. Part of me refused to inquire about why they couldn't better equip me with answers to age-old questions. What were they going to church for if they couldn't answer some of the basic questions about the doctrine of the church they belonged to for many years? I hit the Bible strong and hard again, reading on a daily basis, hoping to find the answers to these images in my mind. Why does God allow such evil things to happen? If God is love and does not rejoice in evil, why is there so much destruction in the world today? I struggled with the concept of an almighty God that would allow such destruction and mass murder as in the struggles in Rwanda, or with Tim McVeigh and the Oklahoma bombing; my life and my grandmother's death; children born into a life of AIDS; cult leaders encouraging their followers to kill; the war on drugs; the years of slavery and today's slavery for blood diamonds; and natural disasters, to name a few.

Why was I having these dreams? I would ask God to pick someone else if He wanted a messenger. I did not like having these nightmares and was angry at God for allowing me to foresee these visions. I was told by a coworker (who was also a pastor of a small church) that I had a gift and God had chosen me to be a minister. Although I never conversed with this pastor, she felt the need to share her vision at a time when it was obvious to others that I was slowly losing my mind. After her statement, I had nothing to say, but knew I didn't want to be a minister. I wanted to be myself. I could not stay focused on anything; my mind wandered in and out of reality. The nightmares were becoming overbearing, and it was hard to distinguish what was reality and what was a dream. The dreams became day and night visions. They also became more frequent and lasted for longer periods of time. What started as periodic dreams turned into my thoughts being consumed. I heard voices, envisioned my death, saw spirits, and suffered from paranoia. I dreaded going to sleep. The dreams became a part of every facet of my life. I would dream of seeing spirits at night; I would see shades of beings wandering around in my brain and in front of my face. I could see millions of them. Sometimes I would see their forms or faces, but it was never clear like a picture, just the forms of the head and body in some cases. I dropped out of college because I could not stay focused on my school work.

I would ponder things all around me and question all existence. It became a full-time obsession to figure out why. Why was there a God? Why was I having these dreams? Why was there so much destruction in the world? Why did God create the angel Lucifer knowing he would turn evil? Why does God allow the devil to commit so much treachery? And most of all, Why am I losing my mind?

After a few months of this, I became distant from everyone I knew and loved. My girlfriend at the time did not want to be around me, and I understood wholeheartedly why. I understood the circumstances, but I must admit that it really hurt because I felt she abandoned me when I was in a very vulnerable state. My younger brother, whom I loved more than any living being, did not want anything to do with me. A heated argument which led to a physical fight, resulted in me trying to stab Levar with a knife. Therefore, I could understand him keeping his distance from me.

I remember going into my father's drawer for a pair of socks one day, and something told me to pull the drawer out. I found a .32 revolver, which fascinated me at first, and I just wanted to fire the gun. I found a few bullets and shot a few rounds into the air in our backyard. I was anxious to shoot the gun. While I was in my delusional state, I took the gun with me and walked around the neighborhood. I went around to the drug spots and found a ride with a few of my brother's friends. I shot at an innocent bystander walking along the street. I could tell that the guys who picked me up were terrified and couldn't wait to get me out of their car. The look in their eyes was of disbelief, and I am sure I had the look of insanity in my eyes. I felt as if my life was a dream. I felt like I was living out some weird fantasy where I was the bad guy. Through all my interactions with family and friends, I remember the expressions on their faces the most. Their expressions told how insane I had become.

Elva, my best friend of all time, still kept in contact. He would always have positive things to say to inspire me to pull myself back together. We had a few discussions about God and the Devil. If it wasn't for him and the brief words of constant encouragement, I don't know if I would have had the strength to go on. I always felt he was there if I needed someone to talk to. Elva was the only person who I felt could relate to my situation and who really was open-minded and sincere about my mindset at the time. My parents were there to support me through this difficult time, even though there were not a lot of conversations between members of the family. I realize today how disheartening it was for my parents to see me in that mental condition. My family thought that I was so out of touch with life and my surroundings that I often heard them talking about me as if I were not there. It was like I had passed away and my spirit was in the room watching my family continue with their lives. I could see the pain in my mother's eyes, as she was at a loss for words and options on what to do with me. I knew she only wanted the best for me, but the only help she could give me was her prayers. I knew I put them through some crazy situations. I was in the midst of a mental breakdown. My family and friends did not know how to cope with this. In my warped thinking I thought I was smart because I was experiencing such spiritual dreams and becoming closer to God. Some mornings I would be up praying for two to three hours outside in the middle of the yard looking crazy! Internally I thought I was beginning to find God. I was getting a glimpse of all God had planned for me, and I was afraid to do anything, to even live life. It's amazing how we build these different worlds in our minds. I would often feel that people were trying to kill me, because I was envisioning my future in fast forward.

After seeing my grandmother's death, I thought God had shown me a sign. I thought that I had the ability to see the future and its destruction. I had to get my life in order in an effort to reach as many people as humanly possible to bring them to God before the end of the world. I truly believed this was my duty from God. The most profound words that aided in my recovery were spoken from my best friend Elva. He said, "Demetrius, don't dwell too much in the life after, but try to live your life today in a way that shows everybody that you are a map to be what God wants you to be." I took those words and turned them into life. I knew I had to learn from my mistakes. No one is perfect, but I would try to live my life to the best of my ability, and that's all I could do. After that, I began my road to recovery. I stopped trying to decipher all the mysteries of the world and concentrated on getting

my life, mind, and friends back. During my mental
instability, Elva proved to be the most vital, inspiring
person in my life. He was the one most willing to help
me throughout my recovery. His friendship through
my hardships proved to me that he would remain a
constant friend in my life. It was the conversations that
meant so much to me. It was the fact that Elva didn't
treat me like a freak, although I wasn't all there. He
took time and treated me with kindness and respect,
and that went a long way when dealing with everyone
who didn't want to be bothered with me.

In an effort to heal my mental deterioration,
my grandfather drove me into the country to see a
voodoo doctor. I don't know if my family believed
that someone "put a root" on me or if they believed
in black magic; Howerver, I traveled in the back seat
of my grandfather's car on the journey to see this man
who was supposed to have the skills to remove this evil
from my body, mind, and soul. On the other hand, I
just prayed he could heal my mind. I don't remember
much about the event except going there and seeing a
barn filled with religious artifacts. I remember feeling
confused and partially uncomfortable. I remember the
man ordering me to put salt water under my bed to
dry up the evil spirits along with a stick or broom. I
was also to read a passage from the Bible whenever I
felt the demons were trying to attack me. I remember
there were nights that I wouldn't go to sleep because I
thought demons were watching, waiting for me to fall
asleep. I couldn't give in to these creatures so I stayed
awake trying to read the Bible. I eventually gave up

as it was such a hard read. The passages were so hard to stay focused on; the verbiage and the story lines were hard to relate to my day-to-day life. I reached out again to family, friends, and church officials, but I didn't learn anything from the meetings.

I remember one day my dad actually advised me to take a ride with my brother and friends to get water from the nearby spring for the house. The water spring is approximately 30 miles from my home, so I rode with my brother and two of his friends in the back seat. I was lost in my own thoughts and didn't much conversation, as I was always observing the miracles of Our Creator. As I looked outside at the clouds, I wished I could fly. It was my destiny to be with God and away from this dreadful world in which we lived. I was tired of all the drugs, killings, death, aches, and pains. I was so looking forward to a life with no stress, the life that God intended for Adam and Eve and for all of humanity to follow. We all fall short of his glory. I was so ready to return to those days to be in God's presence. When we reached the springs, I remained to myself as my brother and his friends gathered their buckets, cartons, and other materials to obtain the water.

After sitting in the car alone for a while, I decided that I wanted to drive the car. I was ready to go home and was tired of sitting at this darn spring. I was getting agitated by the minute. I saw that my brother left the keys in the car, so I was able to walk my way around to the driver's seat and hopped in. My brother and his friends tried to advise me not to drive in my mental condition. They tried to get me out of the driver's seat, but I wasn't having it. I pulled off and left everyone. I stopped a few yards away and gave them one last opportunity to catch a ride home with me. They reluctantly got into the vehicle and complained from the time they got into the car. They pleaded their case as to why I didn't deserve to drive. I wasn't having it and continued to drive, racing past everyone in front of me. We all headed back to OB, with their fate was in my hands. It was raining outside, yet I was speeding with no concern for my life or anyone else's. As I made a steep turn doing 90 miles an hour, I lost control of the vehicle. I recall everyone being ejected from the car and lying on the side of the road.

I got on my hands and knees and prayed fervently to Jesus. I didn't get off the ground for anything. I was on my knees for what seemed at least an hour, ignoring everyone: the highway patrolmen, my brother and friends, onlookers and my parents. My brother cursed at me and yelled at my father about not wanting to take me with him on this trip in the first darn place. Levar felt like our father put his life in jeopardy by having crazy go for the ride. I remember my brother and father arguing about the accident, but it all seemed surreal as I watched in disbelief. I thanked God again for having His protecting hand over my life. I was perplexed as to why God continued to bless me. What did He have in store for me? The accident didn't' completely change me, but there were two defining moments in my life that truly made me take God seriously. The first was my suicide attempt. The second was my time spent in jail.

I was home alone, which was common, since no one wanted to be around a crazy person who could see demons. I stayed inside most of the day and deserted my friends and family. I was an outcast in every sense of the word. In addition, I was at the lowest point in my life, with no glimpse of return. I had given up on ever returning to the fun, loving, spiritual person I once was. I went to my father's dresser and retrieved his .32 revolver, made sure that it was fully loaded, and looked down the barrel of the gun. I said a special prayer to my God. I asked Him to prove to me that he had plans for my life. I challenged God's ability and commanded that He show me his real existence. I vowed to believe in Him if I could get some confirmation that He is real.

I put the gun to my head, pulled back the trigger, and said one last time with anger in my voice, "God, if you have any plans for my life, if there is any reason I should not pull this trigger and meet my maker, give me a sign right this minute." I was in tears because I so desired to have meaning; I desired that He show me what He needed of me. I wished that life were more than life and death. I knew it had to be more than waking up and going to sleep. I wanted to know there had to be more to this life than what I had been doing. I knew the pain I was experiencing through this breakdown had to have a meaning. As I made this final plea to my Lord God, at that very second, I heard a car door slam. I looked outside, and there was my mother coming home from work. I knew at that moment, and put the gun back inside the drawer.

I went to the door to see my mother get out of the car from work. I thanked God for answering my prayers. I thanked God for allowing me to envision the outcome if my mother found my brains all over the floor when she got home. I thought about the effects the decision to commit suicide would have had on my mother. As I reflected on her face, God laid this all on my heart in a quick flash. That was one of the first signs that I recalled of God working in my life. I struggled with the thought of just listening to Him. I was unsure which voice was that of God sometimes. I was scared, but I knew He would lead me where He wanted me to go. Since this time, I have been on, and off the mark, God has set for my life, but I still believe He has something for me.

Chapter 7

Vacation to Probation

My family decided to let me go to Atlanta with my cousin Tray for a few days. He had been asking me to come to Atlanta. My cousin felt that a different environment might help me mentally. My uncle Nick, Tray's father, took me to Atlanta. When I first arrived, I immediately felt an uneasy feeling. I remember there were just so many different people in the house that I felt a little uncomfortable. I immediately felt bad vibes in the house and saw many demons in the room. I hated to see my uncle leave, but I wanted to try something new and get out of my comfort zone. I was still having such an issue getting back to my normal self, so I tried not to give way to the fear of doing something different. I stuck the uncomfortable feeling aside and tried to enjoy myself. Tray tried to make me feel comfortable while I was there. Tray showed me where I could put my stuff and introduced me to his crew.

It felt good to be away from home, as I felt trapped in Orangeburg. I hadn't left the house in months and was getting so bored being at home all the time by myself. It just so happened to be Football Classic weekend in Atlanta. Traditionally, this was a mini-rivalry between South Carolina State University and Georgia Southern. I remember sitting in the apartment zoned out. I was surrounded by guys smoking weed and drinking liquor. I had stopped all of that after my grandmother's death and was trying to live a Christ-like life. I had been saved after my grandmother's death. Between the breakdown and being saved, my spirit wasn't at ease around my friends any longer. Today wasn't any different, miles away from home but in the same old environment. I didn't feel comfortable here with all of the illegal activity. I prayed that Jesus would save me from the breakdown that I was experiencing. More importantly that He would allow me to change my old ways. Being around this behavior again didn't help. I felt so out of touch with what was going on there that I remember just wanting to go home after the first day, but I was dropped off and had to wait a week until my ride came to pick me up. The days seemed long, as it consisted of waking up, scrounging up something to eat, and watching the guys play video games all day long.

I was bored out of my mind one day and decided I was going to get out of the house. I took the Marta train just to get out. I rode the train until it wouldn't go anymore. I realized after I got off the train that I didn't know where I was. I was completely lost. I called my cousin from a pay phone and asked him how to get back to the apartment. I had limited funds; I was in a new city, absolutely out of my mind, a mental wreck. I ended up riding that train from one side of Atlanta to the other. I enjoyed looking at several different neighborhoods; the train ran from affluent neighborhoods to drug-infested neighborhoods. I finally made it back to the apartment and was pooped after a long day of riding and getting lost.

The day my life changed I remember waking up to see two cops looking at me. Now, I haven't always been a law-abiding citizen. During my life, I have witnessed several dirty cops. I already had a negative outlook of all police officers. I truly despised them, and now here they were in the apartment, which was a violation in my book. I stood up, and the officer asked for my ID. I, in turn, asked for his ID. "Why are you here?" I asked. "What are you doing in here?" I was asked again for my I.D. I refused to give them my ID without receiving an explanation as to why they were in the apartment in the first place. One officer placed his hand around my arm as if he were going to arrest me. The other officer had his hand on his gun and began to assist his partner. I jerked away from him and told him to keep his fucking hands off me. He grabbed me again, and I punched him in the face as we wrestled to the ground. The other officer then jumped in, and the two subdued me. They took me to DeKalb County Jail for obstruction and assault on a police officer. While being booked and processed, I retaliated against anyone and everyone I could reach.

Every time someone came within arm's reach, I tried to knock them out. It wasn't easy sitting in that jail cell like a caged animal. I was so full of anger for unjustly being there. I felt I was being punished for some unknown reason. All I could think about was being singled out as a young black male in America. However, a thought flashed that I was there for all the other crimes I've committed for which I wasn't caught. I quickly turned all my anger toward anyone with a badge. I was determined to channel my emotion toward anybody other than myself. When an officer came and dropped off food for lunch, I lunged at him and began to drag him to the floor. I swung with all my might as the blood rushed through my veins. With each swing, I tried to cause as much bodily harm to the individual as possible. After, what seemed a split second, I saw the detective who had put the handcuffs on me approaching. I reacted like a caged animal as that was my feeling at the time. I saw others rushing to aid the officer, with billy clubs in their hands. I hit him one last time below the belt, to make sure I left my mark. Well, that was my last punch thrown. My cell was bombarded by police officers. I remember getting an elbow to my jaw. I was hit in the head with a blackjack. I saw the stun gun electricity hit my flesh, and that was when I fell to the ground. I was kicked and stomped by the officers for several minutes, as I folded myself into a cradle position until it was all over. As I lay on the cold concrete floor in my own blood, saliva, and urine, I felt anger, confusion, and a sense of being lost. I lay there for several hours as correctional officers walked past my cell pointing and making comments about the incident.

At this point, I felt the entire penal system was against me, and the only thing I could do was be an animal, locked in a cage. I felt like an animal. I felt the raw, animalistic side of any human being under the worst conditions. I remember pissing in the interview room, cursing through the solid glass at the people on the other side watching. After punching and assaulting the second correctional officer, they sent the goon squad after me and tasered me again. The jolt of the electric voltage through my body was numbing. I felt my heart beating hard and fast. My heart felt as if it was coming out of my chest and it caused an unusual pain. Thereafter, I was being kicked, spit on, and punched by the officers at the county jail. Again, I found myself lying on the cold concrete floor, unable to move. My body felt numb. My back, head, and face were in so much pain. The pain rushed through my body. Pure anger crept into my mind and flowed through my veins, giving me energy. A few hours later, I was talking to the magistrate judge about my assault charges I'd committed while in the county. I must admit everything felt so surreal, the makeshift courtroom and only officers. It took eight officers to escort me into the court session. While waiting on him to do his job, I snapped. I called the judge a racist cracker, told him to suck my private, fuck him and fuck the entire penal system. I gave everyone the middle finger in the courthouse, and dared the judge to do his job! I was so full of rage at the events that had transpired that I wanted to fight. I wasn't good at expressing my emotions and didn't know how to express my frustrations or communicate in a productive manner. I was found guilty and escorted back to my holding tank. I remember images of the officers and their battalions striking my head. Police officers from all areas were rushing to my cell to kick or spit on me. Every officer on duty wanted to whip my ass. I remember feeling humiliated as I heard the words guilty. What does that mean? How am I guilty? I should have never been in jail in the first place.

I honestly think this was the moment that helped put me back on track mentally. After that high voltage surged through my body, I seemed to start to get my senses back. My sanity seemed renewed. I didn't have dreams about the demons any longer, but I was scared as I reflected on one of my first dreams from my breakdown. I saw myself in jail and prison. It dawned on me that God was real and showing me clear signs that He was real. I began to accept my fate as divine purpose, because it appeared I was supposed to go through this. Although I wasn't instantly cured, within the week, I was a heck of a lot better mentally than I had been prior to the incident in the county jail. Maybe it was the arrest, or maybe it was the beat down the officers gave me. No one knows but God. All I know is that I was starting to see a difference in my mindset, and I was so appreciative for that. It was what I dreamed and prayed for nightly - a return to a solid, stable mind state, a mentality of peace and clarity. My parents came to see me from behind the glass bars. They told me not to hit anyone else and to stay calm, as they were working on getting me out of there. It was at that point that I felt my family was in my corner working for me and on my behalf. When I was locked up, I felt everyone had forsaken me, especially my God. The way all this went down had made me question why God would allow me to go through this and why. Why would He put me through such an ordeal? What Father would do such a thing to their kids? I didn't get in any more trouble after that day. I was released on bond a few hours later. I felt it was the best thing in my life, walking out of jail. It felt so refreshing, so humane. I felt as if I were given a new lease and outlook on life. From that point forward, I was determined never to see the inside of a cell again. When I got home, all I wanted to do was put everything behind me. I wanted to wish it all away. I just wanted it to disappear, although I knew that wasn't in God's plan. I had to answer for the assault cases. I racked up three assault charges while in jail. However, I was out on bond until my court date.

Chapter 8

The Road to Recovery

When I returned to South Carolina, all my attention was on starting anew. After a few days of getting my mind focused and getting my friends caught up with the drama, I met with Elva. He instructed me to get a job. The ironic part was being in charge of a group home of mental health clients. I worked third shift and enjoyed what I did, which was nothing much. I walked the perimeter of the house, to ensure no clients were out of their rooms and walking around at night. I prepared food and assisted with the day-to-day operations of the group home. I cleaned, dressed, and bathed the male clients. God conveniently allowed me to work with people who had a mental disability. This fit right in for me. I felt God was again working on my behalf as I was beginning to get myself together. I still wasn't at 100%, but I was stable enough to hold down a job again. I had found the job through my best friend, and I was working with teenagers through 60-year-olds. It was a very rewarding job which I truly enjoyed. I realized how much I truly enjoyed helping people. I could do this forever; the kids were very smart, although they were mentally challenged. These individuals had very distinct personalities. They were high-functioning kids, which enabled some of them to dress themselves, feed themselves, etc. Some of them loved to dance and sing to music, and some loved to be alone. I had kids with anger management problems and some that were just plain perverts. I was very comfortable with them all and felt this was a renewing of my spirit. I viewed it as a time of self-reflection. It was also a look into what my friends and family had to endure with me to a degree. As I looked at the special needs children, I felt so much understanding and compassion. I had been where they currently were; I could relate to how they felt and how they were viewed. I was very compassionate with each of my clients. I felt the need to protect them and show them an unconditional love that their own families didn't show them. I could remember the feelings of abandonment from friends and loved ones. I knew how it felt to be misunderstood, to look for meaning in your life through connections with others. I made sure that my interactions with my clients were always genuine.

I was out on bond and periodically during the year had to drive back and forth to Georgia to attend court. My lawyer finally came to my parents and me with a plea bargain. After a whole year, I asked my lawyer if this were a good deal. He explained that assault on an officer carried a 20-year sentence for each count, and I had three of them. My lawyer added that the state had many eye witnesses and sworn testimonies from nurses, judges, and several officers about my behavior. In addition, the state would paint a very negative picture of me, my attitude and actions. He spoke about my antics and my racist and defamatory comments made to the judge. The judge wanted to know if I were a black nationalist, as I had made many references about racial disparities. My lawyer claimed that if he continued to take it to trial, I could get 60 years. He then confirmed that this was the best offer. He explained to me how the penal system worked, and that I would be out in less than a year, under the first offender act. As hard as I was, I was so naïve to the way the penal system operated. I thought all lawyers were like the old show *Matlock*, the type of lawyer who would fight tooth-and-nail for their clients. I asked my parents their thoughts. They advised me to take the offer, so I did. I pleaded guilty to assault and was given a five-year sentence: four years in prison and one-year probation. I truly didn't understand what I had gotten myself into. I knew I was wrong for my actions, and my poor decision had landed me right where I was. After my sentencing, I was given one month to get my affairs in order and was required to turn myself in, October 1995. This was a long hard month for me. I immediately returned to work and gave them my two weeks' notice. I apologized and informed them of my actions prior to my employment. I was so thankful for the opportunity they had given me, and I wanted them to understand that, upon my return, I wanted to come back if they would have me. The next two weeks were a true test, as I was given every opportunity to run and avoid prison. I had several connections in the streets and probably could have lived on the run for years without detection. I had connections throughout the East Coast, and all I had to do was call in a few favors.

My last day free was spent with close friends and family. My cousin Tray had a party at his house. Everyone asked why I was turning myself in and said that I should flee to New York to avoid doing time. Everyone had an opinion as to my future. They said I was a fool for turning myself in. I reflected on the premonition I had of being in jail. God had shown me to face my demons head on. I told everyone I would be back, and that I would be stronger when I got out. I left my going away party early that night. I needed some time alone to process my thoughts and feelings. I could not sleep when I got home. I could only reflect on my life and the things I had done to get to this point in my life. I thought to myself that this life has to be so much more than what I was living. There had to be more! That was the last thing I thought about as I finally closed my eyes.

The next morning I was up and unusually content with what I was about to face. As I traveled from Orangeburg to Atlanta, I just stared out the window, in and out of reality, thinking about this twist of fate and my future. My parents were lost in their own thoughts. I tried to make conversation throughout the three-hour ride, but there really wasn't anything to talk about.

Once we were at DeKalb County Jail, it looked huge from the outside. We didn't have buildings like that in Orangeburg. I looked at it with fear, knowing that I would be trapped in this place. Part of me wanted to run home. I began to think about the statements my cousins had made prior to today. "Man, run. Don't turn yourself in."

Why turn myself in? Let them come and get me. The thought started to cross my mind. I decided to gather my strength and what little sense of pride I had left. I grabbed the little things I was able to bring with me: my bag of white cotton boxers and T-shirts, soap, toothbrush etc. As I said my goodbyes and the officer escorted me in the direction I needed to go, I refused to look back. I accepted my fate like a man. I told everyone that I loved them and swore that I would see them again when I was free. I made that promise to myself that I would get out of this one day. I knew I would be a free man again.

I know it was the best decision to face my actions. I was scared as the devil after looking at prison movies. I was terrified about what my future held for me. I felt at the time that I was no longer the violent, angry teenager I had been prior to my release. I had learned my lesson and didn't need to do any prison time. I had been living a productive life and hadn't gotten into any trouble. Why couldn't we just wipe the slate clean? I was an immature little kid. As I prepared myself mentally for the prison life I was about to face, I thought about all the things I desire out of this life before I died, and the thing that stood out the most was a family. I wanted a wife who loved me; I wanted a house that I could call my own; I wanted kids who respected me and whom I could love and play with and watch grow into fruitful adults. I would teach them all that I had learned and experienced so they would not go through the same things I did. I would pour my heart into their growth and development. I would give them unconditional love that I wished and dreamed of. The kind of love that I had never experienced but knew was possible. I would be the best father anyone could possibly have or be.

I couldn't remember when I turned into this thug character, this alter ego personality of mine. I reflected on this, and it always came back to alcohol, gin and liquor. Whenever I drank gin, it would make me sin. The dark side came out. That alter ego - careless, carefree, reckless, potentially violent, the person who truly doesn't give a crap. I have found even today that when I drink hard liquor, I become someone I don't care to be. That is one reason I have decreased the amount of hard liquor I drink. I have found that beer satisfies my alcoholic taste buds but still allows me to be myself without the extra influence. I am able to control the alcohol and not allow the alcohol to control me. I remember an old saying, "Don't let the liquor control you; you control the liquor." Do what you can handle; know your limits.

The first year was the hardest for me in prison. It took so much out of me to be around so many people who had committed so many heinous crimes. Reality hit and with it came feelings of me being overwhelmed.

74

Every one of my 'cellies' or roommates was a murderer. I thought I was a bad ass, but I was filled in a box full of brothers who have done way more things than me. I would listen to some of the things my cellmates had done, and I thought to myself that this was not the life I wanted to live. The gangs, the nation, the Arian nation, Muslims, bikers, pedophiles - it was such a disturbing place to be. As I reflected on my life, I had been in the military and college; now look where I was! I shouldn't be here! I thought back on all the bad choices I had made that ultimately landed me here. "We are all the sum of our decisions." I cried for the first time in many years.

There is nothing like a grown man crying like a baby. I could not believe how I had ruined my life. I thought back to entering the prison for the first time. As myself and other inmates get escorted to our pods, there is complete silence as many watched. There are inmates playing chess or playing cards, watching TV, huddled together talking, some taking showers, and others just chilling. A big dorm around a bunch a men has become my temporary living space. Once I entered my cell, without looking back, I will never forget that final moment; the cell doors closing. As I lay in my bunk bed, my roommate told me he cried many nights and encouraged me to get it out. He was in for murder and would never see home again. He was 18. His words were like therapy to me. I needed to hear it to allow me to let it out without any worries. The holidays were the hardest times to be away from loved ones. I met some real guys in there, though. We shared war stories over a hot cup of "Joe" or coffee, smoked black and mild cigars, and reminisced. There were nights that we would stay up until daybreak talking about crazy stuff we did on the streets. Lots of us played cards, basketball, chess, etc., to keep our minds off the fact that we were slaves to this penal system. Some found God in prison, which helped them deal with their own inner demons. I found several religions that I had never heard of before life in prison, like Islam and Wicca. I was open-minded to others' religions and learned as much as possible. However, religion has always been a hard thing for me to get my head around. I think the same God that created everyone with different genetic codes and fingerprints, and who made each snowflake different would have other religions or more than one way to reach Him. I believe that just as God created different languages at the tower of Babel, He created different ways and languages to reach His people. In doing so, when He called His people, they would respond in their native tongues. Also, in my studies of different religions, I realized a lot of them have the same core view. Praise the one God of the world, live your lives right, and treat your fellow man fairly and kindly. I believe God doesn't make mistakes. I believe God has a plan for all of our lives. I believe He put us through trials and tribulation because there is a lesson to be learned from the experience. Sometimes, innocent people have to die just to save a sinner, someone who's hard to reach. This was something I struggled with at one time in my life. Why did God allow kids to die? Why do good people die young? Why do bad things happen to good people? I know God makes everything work for the greater good of His will. I reflect on how I wound up in prison. I was no one's angel, and I did a lot of things that I was not proud of. I knew I deserved to be in prison. Today I am a more positive person. I try my best to help people. I have a good heart and try to teach people from my life experiences. I try to help people avoid some of the traps that I experienced in my life or fell victim to. I have been told that I have touched several people's lives through volunteering at the county jails and through my interactions with youth at work. It's so refreshing to hear these comments from people.

I enjoy being able to make a difference in people's lives. I have become someone people respect and a model for them to live their lives after. God knows I am no saint; I have a lot more growth and potential, but I have come a long way and am proud of everything God has done to me to make me who I am today. I thank Him for the people He has placed in my life that enable me to continue to grow and become the man He expects and knew I would be. I look forward to God continuing the good work He has started in me until the day of Christ.

I Have a New Attitude

Chapter 9

My Love - My Wife

I was working at a call center called Cendant where we booked reservations for Howard Johnson Hotels and Avis. I walked through the aisles of the large call center filled with cubicles, computers, and people ranging in age. Walking through any call center, you feel like you are a piece of meat on the chopping block because all eyes are on you. You feel the stares of everyone as you move throughout the center. I remember taking a large breath and thinking to myself how beautiful she was. At that moment, I made a mental note of this young lady, and knew deep in my loins that I wanted her to myself forever. I remember thinking I need her. After the initial thought, I found myself mesmerized by her natural beauty. I thought about the day I first laid eyes on her face. Her skin tone was caramel in color. Her lips were full and just the right size with a smile that is able to brighten any room. Her coke bottle frame made my heart flutter. I immediately said to myself, "I bet she is stuck on herself; conceited to the core. She seemed to carry herself with her head in the air, as if everything revolved around her." I killed the thought of speaking to her and went about my business.

Over the next few weeks, every time I saw this girl, my body had this funny feeling, as if it yearned to have her. Now, I have never been one to be superficial and base decisions solely on a person's outer appearance, but each time I saw her, I desired to have her physically, mentally, and emotionally. These feelings were new to me. After being locked in a cage with hundreds of men for several years, I desired a woman who I could settle down with and begin to build a family. Throughout the next couple of weeks of my training class, I would look to find her, if for nothing else, to see her beauty. I remember saying to myself that only about three women in the entire call center looked good, but in my eyes, there was only one who stood out, had the personality, and carried herself in a manner that made me want to get to know her. That was Jacqueline. I wanted to know if she had any brains to go along with the pretty face. I needed to know if this young lady was indeed grounded.

After what seemed an eternity, I was out of training and on the sales floor to work my normal shift. Jackie worked first shift and I worked second, so I only had an hour to get her attention. I sat near her and her crew and made it my business to introduce myself to her. I knew with Jackie I had to take my time and have the right approach. Throughout the next couple of weeks, I would speak or acknowledge her presence but had no major dialogue. Her cousin was the one who really made it happen when she paired us together for a date. We began to speak about different types of food. She liked seafood, but I never had it, nor had I eaten at Red Lobster, which was where we decided to go on our very first official date. Jackie made it known that we would be "going Dutch" and that she would pay for her portion of the food. She didn't want to give me a misconception that she was dependent on any man or that this was a date. After all, the terminology for dating in this small town meant screwing. Jackie met me at my parents' house, and she drove us to the restaurant. The nearest Red Lobster was about a 40 minute drive. I remember being so excited, like a little kid. This was really happening. The most beautiful girl I have ever known had picked me up to take me to dinner. Man was God good. I pinched myself in the car, because I was thinking this had to be a dream. The whole time, I was concentrating on how not to mess up this date. Hell, I was 26, and I had never gone on a real first date before, so I would probably do something that I wasn't supposed to. I tried to keep the conversation light, since I was so nervous inside. We did a lot of small talk along the way about the weather, being down South, our parents, etc.

Once we arrived at the restaurant, I made sure I did the things I had learned from watching TV like opening the doors, giving thanks for everything, giving special compliments on my date's appearance, etc. When we were seated, we had the perfect waiter. He had a lot of energy and created a very relaxing experience for us. I will always remember what Jackie wore, because the waiter kept calling her "orangey." She wore a pair of off-white dress slacks with a cantaloupe-colored silk shirt that she accented with a scarf. Our date went well. We had a few drinks; we ate and talked about anything and everything that night. I was at a point in my life where I wanted desperately to avoid contact with males. Being in prison surrounded by men for years had killed my desire to associate with or hang with any males at all. I realized in prison that I had so much to live for. I wanted to have a family, to own a home, and to have children that I could raise and teach life skills that I learned through experience. I was ready for a committed relationship. I was in a three year relationship in the past, which didn't end well and left a sour taste in my mouth about females in general. I allowed my past to dictate my future, and it hindered me from opening up to the women in the past and giving them 110%. I was determined that I would not allow that to happen again with this young lady.

We were in the restaurant almost two hours, and it was the best experience I ever had with any woman. I was all smiles inside. I drove us back home, and we continued to talk all the way. I felt I had found someone who could really understand some of the things that I had been through. Jacqueline was a very good listener. She was very receptive of my feelings and asked questions about things that were not very clear to her from our conversations. She offered suggestions on things I could do to have a better relationship with my family. I thought after that first night together that I had found a pretty face with a brain, as well. It felt so good to have someone who didn't hold my past deeds against me.

As the relationship progressed, we became sexually active. This date was special as well, as I felt that awkward feeling for the first time since I had lost my virginity. These feelings overwhelmed me with so many emotions that our first time didn't last very long. I was so embarrassed. My pride just deflated quickly. We talked about it, and I was given another opportunity to redeem myself. Jackie and I spent a lot of our time together, whether it was on the phone or at work. We took personal time off from work so we could do things together like go to the Battery in Charleston, SC. I had never heard of the Battery. However, Jackie knew about this scenic area, since she lived in New York. We spent endless hours in the park talking about anything and everything. During our conversations, we both discovered we had similar business interests and could eventually work together to bring our dreams to light. I never told her at first, but I knew that I loved her and had to have this girl. Jackie was my breath of fresh air and all that I had prayed for while I was down. Six months later, God had begun his work in my life and I was on the road to fulfilling my dreams. I can finally "exhale."

Marriage Isn't Easy

Chapter 10

When Love Is not Enough

After Jackie and I dated for approximately four months, we decided we wanted to move in together. We couldn't get enough of each other and wanted to be together all the time. We were adults, and this wasn't an extraordinary request. We decided we were going to tell our parents, so we got them all together at Jacqueline's mother's house. I remember the day as if it were yesterday. Jackie's mother was dead set against it and insinuated that I wasn't good enough for her daughter. My parents weren't as cynical, but they let me know that they felt we were moving too fast. Now, both Jackie and I are stubborn, so once we had made up our minds that we were going, there was nothing anybody could say to keep us in Orangeburg - period.

We moved to Charlotte in May 2000. I woke up the morning of October 9, 2000, and told Jacqueline I wanted to get married. We planned to get married at the courthouse in my hometown. Although we did not have the funds for a wedding or to plan a reception, Jacqueline still wanted to dress appropriately for the occasion. My wife-to-be and I went shopping for a dress and suit prior to our union together. After we had purchased her dress, I noticed some Nike Air Force One sneakers on sale and bee-lined to Footlocker. I wanted to wear the sneakers so bad that I kept them on and put my old sneakers inside the box, then took the box to the register. At the register, the cashier had another box of sneakers sitting on the desk. She lost track of which box was mine and ended up scanning a cheaper pair of sneakers and placing them in the bag with the receipt. As the cashier handed me the bag, Jacqueline informed her that she had rung up the wrong pair of sneakers. I tried to get her to hush, but it was too late. When we left the store, I cussed Jackie out for telling the cashier about her error. Jacqueline stood her ground and preached to me about being honest and living right. I could care less about her spiel. After all, I could have gotten an extra pair of sneakers and saved $30, since the sneakers the cashier rang up were cheaper. I was truly pissed and recall this being our first argument concerning this subject, but there were many more to come. *(I didn't realize then that I still had to break the hustler mindset)*. Regardless, I brushed off our differences and applied for our marriage license that afternoon. Since Jackie was under 25 years of age, we had to come back exactly 24 hours later to be married. October 10, 2000: Our true journey begins.

After moving to Charlotte on blind faith, I got a job the first day. I was out in the streets selling books and toys to people for cash. The job paid daily, and it was something until I was able to find a better job. I walked several miles a day to hustle those books. Every evening when I got home, I applied to different jobs in hopes of getting something better. Shortly after, I found a job at Sears in the electronics department. Having a street degree in sales, I knew this would be easy for me. Things were beginning to look up for us. It wasn't easy, as nothing in life ever is, but we took it day by day. It didn't take long for the arguments to start, and that's when we realized we were in over our heads. There was so much we still didn't know about each other. We had only been together a total of eight months before we were married. We were still learning each other.

Jackie had a daughter prior to our marriage whom I eagerly accepted as my own. I knew I wanted a family and knew that this level of commitment would be exactly what I needed to get myself together. I knew being a good father was something I had dreamed about in prison. I felt everything was happening for a reason; I felt God was blessing me with all the things I asked of Him. He knew the responsibility of raising a family was what I needed to transform me into a man. I needed a strong woman who would support my growth, overlook my flaws, and push me past my comfort zone. I found everything I needed in my wife. She was perfect for me. God is truly a matchmaker. In addition, our daughters make each day worth it.

Our children are the driving force that continues to give us that extra push to do more for ourselves and them. We have two beautiful girls who have always inspired me to have more and do more for them and their future.

The firstborn is Jaclyn; our artistic child. Jaclyn has such a big personality, wrapped in such a very small package. Jaclyn has the ability to manipulate the best of them with her quiet analytic demeanor. She's striving to become an actress and business owner, and has been in acting classes for the last four years. She is good at truly immersing herself in her character and gives it her personality. She has also written her own play and performed it in class. The creative spirit is refreshing, and it encourages her to think out of the box, which is so crucial for our young and new generation. I truly enjoy having conversations with her and look forward to seeing her on the big screen or teaching other children the art and skill of drama.

Daijah is the baby and hasn't quite made up her mind what she wants to do just yet. She is very affectionate and has the ability to win over everyone because of her heart. Her desire and commitment to family was recognized early. Daijah always wanted to cuddle and be under someone. As Daijah grew, her affection has grown to include one-on-one time with her parents and grandparents.

There were times during our marriage that tested my being. It appeared that women can test your every fiber and men as well I guess. I found myself in arguments with my wife about everything. She would find things to argue about all the time. I felt that I could do nothing right in her eyes. From washing the dishes, to vacuuming the carpet, to fixing or doing odd jobs around the house, there was always something that was negative. I thought she was the most negative person I knew. I quickly realized that I could not go back and forth with my wife, because she was very skilled at remembering the faults of others all too well, which I later called "historical." I found that she could easily recall my issues like a historian recalls ancient artifacts. She would throw things in my face that I didn't even remember. I felt she was a sponge of hatred at times, and her delivery stung like a viper. Some of the things she said could really mess with the psyche of my being. I had to pray daily to ensure that I wouldn't lose focus on the bigger picture that we were going to be together. We needed to learn each other. I was patient, and I knew that we would get it together soon.

In hindsight, I came into the marriage with so much baggage. I was a convicted felon with bad credit, I didn't have a history of respect for women, and I didn't have a clue on how to be a responsible man. I had lived for many years in my maleness, but I learned from my wife how to be a responsible man. I realize today how frustrating it has been for my wife, dealing with my mess. To be in a relationship with a man whose potential you see, yet he lacks the foundation. As I developed, and grew, the lessons I learned from my wife became blatant. The changes were so apparent to my family and friends. I could tell by the way I viewed things that my philosophy on life had changed. The way I viewed excuses my family and old associates made about their lack of success was immediately confronted by ways to improve their situation. I recalled when I would sit and agree with them about how all the forces of the world were against them, but today, I realize we hold ourselves back from 99% of our success. I realize today that my wife had to develop and harness that potential she saw in me. I know that I was a hard nut to crack, and it took patience, constant correction, and my will to want to make the necessary changes. My wife would get so pissed at me about my lack of management of our finances. My parents didn't teach me about money. If I needed money for anything and they had it to give, they did just that with no message or spiel like my wife often has with our girls. They didn't teach me how to save or invest money, nor did I have a true concept of its value. The key thing that pissed Jackie off was my lack of knowledge about credit. Lord, some days I just didn't want to hear it, but I knew she would never misguide me. I always kept in mind through all her anger that she had my best interest at heart. I was accustomed to cash, as it was king in the world I lived in. This was a very hard and long lesson, learning to be a man instead of a cocky male trying to look like "I had a pot to piss in and a window to throw it out of". Many days, my wife made me feel like the change in my pocket wasn't worth shit, and the truth is, she was right. I always kept a job and made fairly decent money, as my wife would often push me to continue to persevere to increase my knowledge and income, and improve my image. As the money increased, so did my spending. My money went to beer or hanging out with friends and family prior to paying my bills. In my life before my wife, leisure was first, and bills got paid if there was money left to do so. This did not sit well with Jackie, and I was often antagonized about my spending any time I brought something new into the house. If I bought a can of beans into the house, she questioned me and wanted to know how much it had cost. Lord, have mercy, my wife means well, but she is the biggest fuss bucket I have ever seen.

The gravity of the responsibilities didn't hit me as it did her. My carefree attitude just added on to the tension and stress. I tried to explain my philosophy to my wife, that God will make a way. I believed that my God didn't bring me this far to leave me now. I was confident that I would be successful in this life, although I didn't know exactly how God was going to do it. My wife was not hearing it, because I was not putting my best foot forward. As the saying goes, "Faith without work is dead." I prayed that God would lighten her load. She wanted me to carry my load, take the driver's seat of our marriage, with all the responsibilities it entailed. I wasn't at that state where I could do that just yet, and it caused major concerns with my wife. I prayed that God would come into her life and give her peace even in the middle of trials and the things I put her through. I hated being the reason for my wife's despair. I felt sometimes that no matter what I did, I would never be able to satisfy my wife. Sometimes

I felt like a little kid yearning for her approval, and no matter what has happened or what I do, I would fall short of her expectations. I had relinquished my individuality for fear it would push her away. The self-struggle and internal yearning for her acceptance had cost me my own individuality. What an expensive lesson! I started to see that I needed to get myself back. I needed to do the things that made me happy. I realized that regardless of how much I loved my wife, I had to do more things for me, to find myself again. I could not please my wife if I was unhappy myself. The quiet yet resilient man she first met was just content with being in her presence and didn't push for more. I decided that I had enough. I decided that she would either love me or leave me. I knew that I wasn't the best man in the world; I knew that I came with a lot of issues. I knew that I was a piece of work. Yet, I also knew that I had a loving spirit. I had the desire to be a better man and a good father, and I was going to be successful. I admitted my wrongs and faults to my wife, but she continued to reject me. Finally, I realized that whatever I did, it would never be enough. No matter what I did, said, or changed, she would never forgive me or allow this marriage to move forward, because she was stuck in the past.

The verbal abuse had escalated. We became increasingly petty. The more we did this, the more we withdrew from each other. I began finding distractions through social media, searching for old connections to the man I once was. I reflected on many childhood friends and began to share my challenges, concerns, and issues with them. I became addicted to social media and spent many hours on the internet to avoid spending time dealing with our true issues. We would sit on the bed next to each other and not say a word, both focused on our Internet distractions.

Jackie would periodically complain about abdominal pain and said that I was making her sick. I didn't pay much attention to her and wrote it off as a mere attempt to cause me additional strife and pain. But one day, I saw the pain on her face. I saw the anguish and suggested she go to the doctor to get a checkup for the pain she complained about. After several incidents, she finally went to the doctor and found out that she had cysts on her ovaries, which caused the pain. The doctor recommended surgery to remove them. I was a wreck. I began to think about all that I had put her through and that maybe I was the cause of her pain. I felt horrible that I had treated her so poorly, and I wanted to do better. In retrospect, prior arguments seemed so trivial. I was so at a loss for words as I thought about the approaching surgery that she would have to go through. I never shared my fears with her. The days leading up to her surgery were the worst. I became even more withdrawn and stayed away from meaningful conversations. I didn't really know what to say to her. I was filled with so much emotion that I didn't say anything. I wanted to let her know I was nervous and scared of losing her. I wanted her to know that I loved her so much and the problems we were having were so childish. I wanted her to say it would all be okay, that we could put our past behind us.

I stayed home from work to go with Jackie to her first appointment after surgery. I needed to hear for myself that her recovery had gone well. I looked at her and subconsciously smiled to myself and said a prayer of thanks to my Creator. It has been just eight days prior that I had been in a hospital waiting for my wife to get through a major surgery. I was nervous, scared, and kind of upset because I couldn't be in the operating room with her. I didn't want her to be out of my sight. I didn't want her to face it alone, and I wanted to be with her every step of the way, watching the procedure if I could. I remember crying when she was wheeled away from me. I remember smelling the palms of my hands for a subtle reminder of her scent from her holding my hands. I can remember my mind racing all over the place for hours not knowing what to expect. I don't want to wish that uncertainty on anyone. It's the worst feeling in the world, fear of the unknown.

Thankfully, the surgery only lasted about two hours, but it felt more like 10 hours had passed before I was able to see her. I tried to immerse myself in my work, although I was supposed to be off. My mind wouldn't allow me to stay focused long enough to get anything done. I paced the waiting area from one side of the hospital to the next, outside and back inside. I scanned every magazine in the waiting area. I cried at the thought of living my life without her in it. I thought of how miserable my life would be. I thought about raising two girls alone without their mother. How would I manage to do such a thing? I remember telling God to remove that thought from my head, because I wasn't prepared for it.

It had been three weeks since my wife's surgery, and strangely everything was going entirely too well. My wife was unusually affectionate. She was behaving like she did when we first started dating, and I was baffled. I didn't know how to take this. At first, I thought it was just because of the surgery, but the change was so drastic it scared the hell out of me. I wasn't used to her holding my hand, rubbing on my arm at night. These were small signs of affection that I had long forgotten about. I knew it was because I had caused my wife so much pain that she had buried her sensitive side toward me. But I was nervous things were going too good to be true. I feared that I couldn't muster up the same sensitivity as she was showing me right then for fear of it being temporary. I love my wife, no question, but there were times I looked into her eyes and wondered when she would revert to what I'm used to. I had experienced this roller coaster long enough to know its up-and-down patterns. I was well aware of Jackie's emotional ride; I was going into it asking how long it would last. In the meantime, I was trying to be as grateful as I could be and I was working to make each day as pleasurable as possible. I hoped, prayed, and wished that it would last, but I asked myself when and how long it would be before the real Jackie would come back. A life of two strangers is what I had sometimes felt between the two of us. Jackie did her thing, and I did mine, like roommates. We tended not to work collectively on almost anything. My wife didn't have my last name; she didn't attempt to get her daughter my last name. This void caused separation within the household in the beginning. My oldest daughter automatically identifies with her mother, because they have the same last name. Subconsciously, that separated Daijah. It pitted Jackie and Jaclyn against Demetrius and Daijah. We didn't pray together or go to church together. We had our own separate accounts, cars, hobbies, etc. I would have loved for us to do something that both of us could enjoy together. It seemed I was always trying to bridge that gap, whether it was bowling because my wife enjoys it or watching a movie she likes. We needed to find things we could do together. I suggested working out, joining a gym, reading books, riding bicycles, and going to a counselor, but nothing became of it. I couldn't do it by myself, and I didn't feel she even cared anymore about what could be done for our marriage. What and how do you fix it, when both parties are not 100% into it anymore? When do you say enough is enough?

Our marriage had been on the brink of destruction from the start. I truly care for this lady and didn't want to give up on our marriage, but she was not willing to continue, so we lived our lives like two strangers. We associated with each other, but at the core, she gave up on this marriage a long time ago. There were a lot of signs for me, but I neglected to pay attention to them. Marriage is such a tricky thing. Sometimes marriage is so beautiful, and other days, so horrendous. It's so frustrating when things are not working well in a marriage. Both parties feel they have done more than the other, and both harbor some type of resentment for the other. It seems as if there are times that we bring out the worst in each other, and for what? You snap at your mate, saying things that truly hurt them. Why? Just to get an emotional response from them because you don't see any emotions at all? I truly hoped and prayed that we could move past this, but it was extremely hard. I felt I deserved better. I felt I had tormented myself long enough. How long should I carry and live *with* my mistakes? How long would I allow my mistakes to dictate my future? Yes, I had messed up royally, but how long would I allow my mistakes to hinder me from God's happiness? I had decided that I had had enough. I needed peace of mind. I needed to be able to have a decent life, and I would have one. I would have loved for it to be with my wife, but it didn't seem that this would be.

There is a very special place in my heart and mind for my wife. There is nothing like having someone who truly cares about your well-being. There is something so very special about someone who wants the best for you and pushes you to excel through all the trials and tribulations that life will throw at you. I think it's crucial to my growth that I had someone like Jackie willing to help steer me in the right direction, being that consistent voice. I also know that this was possible because of God's will to make a difference in my life and the potential and vision my wife saw in me from the very beginning. It was something I was unable to see in myself. I saw the direction my wife was trying to push me in, and I saw that it would be beneficial to all involved. I run into people who are not willing to do anything different in their lives but wonder why they get the same results. In essence, we expect a different outcome yet fail to change our current behaviors.

Part II – By Jacqueline Irick

Jacqueline's Influence

My Passion to Influence:

Becomes My Trial and My Testimony

I always believed in giving a second chance to others, as I know that I have gone down the wrong path a time or two. No one wants to be constantly reminded of their transgressions or viewed in the same light, when making the steps toward change. The ignorance of others and the unwillingness to influence "lost souls" is the result of repeat offenses and an unchanged lifestyle. By all means, we cannot save all, but we can try to reach many. If we did not have positive people, those willing to help others, spiritual leaders, angels, the unselfish and the visionaries, what would this world be? Ignorance and selfishness are the downfall of any man, to include one's self. Why concern myself? It's not me, nor will it ever be me. Why help, when their problem is not my problem? If every religious leader had the same way of thinking, lives would never be changed nor saved. Just as sinners attend church and constantly work toward change, criminals can walk the street without a conviction. Guilty is not the man in jail any more than the man walking free; he has yet to be caught.

Chapter 11

Starting Our Life Together & The Family Drama

I love my husband with all my heart. Like every marriage there are ups and downs. It would not be right for me to simply talk about the highs because that would not help anyone get through the lows. I believe what the Bible says about marriage:

> Therefore shall a man leave his father and his mother, and shall cleave unto his wife: and they shall be one flesh.
>
> Genesis 2:24

For a long time my husband struggled with following these instructions. His unwillingness to address issues or speak up on my behalf created an atmosphere of resentment and disrespect. Some of our issues began early in the relationship. When Dee and I lived together his mother would call and say, "Is Demetrius there?" There was no hello, how are you doing? Although, there was not much conversation with his father, at least Mr. Irick always spoke to me and attempted to hold a conversation before talking to his son. The disregard from his mother ended after we were married. However, by this time I was no longer concerned with building a bond and made no efforts to make small talk; I just handed Dee the telephone.

I realized after getting married that our upbringing was totally opposite. Even the little things that seemed common knowledge to me became a source of daily frustration. For example, I was taught not to walk into someone's home; stand at the door and wait to be invited in. Upon entering, sit where directed and don't walk through the home unless given a tour. When given an invitation to a family gathering, ask permission of the hostess before inviting additional company. It is always appropriate to take something for the host, or as my mother would say, "Never walk with your hands swinging". Do not wear out your welcome by staying more than two or three hours and stopping by unannounced. Respect a person's bedroom as a sacred place, and never enter that room unless invited. These principles along with many other rules were embedded in my brain at a young age by my mother. As the saying goes, "No two households run the same," and there was confusion in our household for many years because of our different family beliefs.

I often felt that the principles and rules that I wanted to enforce in our household were disregarded (with much assistance from my husband). I often asked Dee to speak to his family about my concerns because it would be best if presented by him. Of course, for almost seven years, nothing was said until I reached my boiling point. By then things were really awkward. Our family functions were limited. I no longer desired to host anything with both sets of grandparents present. I intentionally did this just to keep the confusion to a minimum and all parties happy. When it comes to the children, the expectation and willingness to come together are different. Sadly, adults do not always model what we preach. I often wished my mother was more forgiving, my father had more of a voice and verbalized his opinions and that my in-laws were more open-hearted.

A marriage between two people can be trying *alone*, but confusion with family or anyone else in the middle of your relationship can create pure chaos. Families often struggle with accepting their child's mate as another son or daughter versus their child's wife or husband. Dee and I have learned to keep our problems at home; as family tends to struggle with separating their personal feelings after all the negative things they've heard. What seems like venting to us appears to our family as degradation and unworthiness of our mate. I struggled in this area, by allowing my emotions to cloud rational thinking, which caused our marriage more harm.

Holidays seemed to be the hardest for (peaceful) family gatherings. Mrs. Irick's most offensive actions were Father's Day 2001. I was pregnant with Daijah when Demetrius called Mr. Irick for Father's Day. Mrs. Irick spoke with Dee for a bit before saying, "I am not going to wish you a happy father's day this year since you are not a father yet." This was repeated to me from Dee's own mouth because he was surprised and appalled by his mother's comment. I watched his jaw drop prior to him abruptly ending his conversation with his mother and sharing with me what she said. Her failure to accept Jaclyn, I found to be highly offensive. As time went on Mr. and Mrs. Irick's actions did not improve. Dee was the only person in our family that was acknowledged for birthdays father's day or contacted via telephone any day. I watched these behaviors for about three years but made sure that I continued to do the right thing. The gifts that I sent were not always acknowledged with a phone call confirming receipt or a mere thank you. If the gift were acknowledged, they talked to Dee and Dee only. Each time I addressed Dee about his parent's he minimized the actions by making excuses. By the fourth year, I developed the concept, "you get what you give". In essence, we only sent gifts or made calls during the holidays, as did they. Over the years, I noticed that Mr. and Mrs. Irick expected their children to honor them but were unwilling to show the same gratitude. By the fifth year, they did not send cards nor initiate phone calls on Mother's Day, Father's Day or birthdays for anyone in our household. If you did not call them, you would not hear from them either. I figured if I showed them their own ignorance my in-laws may see the errors of their ways. For instance, my in-laws sent a gift for the holidays which I intentionally did not call them to acknowledge. However, we sent them a gift around the same time and had not received a phone call, as well. About a month later, Dee and I visited for the weekend. Mrs. Irick asked me did we receive the gift they sent for the holidays. I replied yes then asked her if she received her gift. She firmly planted her feet to the floor in reaction to my comment. This situation was a clear indicator to me that they knew better but refused to do better.

In the midst, of our marital problems arose issues between both sets of parents. My parents called the children and asked to keep them during the summers. My in-laws did not. My in-laws only expressed interest when they knew our children were in my parents care. My mother started taking the children over to my in-laws so that they would not feel left out. I did not agree because they did not show the same genuine interest as my parents. Once my mother stopped taking the kids over to their home, the nitpicking began. My father-in-law expressed concerns of feeling slighted and told my parent's that the grandchildren should know and spend time with both sets of grandparents. However, no one was stopping them. Eventually, I had to speak to my in-laws about their behaviors since my parents were trying to remain neutral and keep the peace. Dee showed no intentions of correcting the problems. Unfortunately, there continues to be a divide between both parents today, and I do not see a bridge being built in the near future. I realized that a lot of these issues could have been minimized if Dee and I addressed them from the very beginning. In addition, more could have been done on my parent's behalf as well to eliminate each situation from spiraling out of control. I am outspoken and prefer to address issues in the infant stages whereas my parents prefer to avoid conflict. We all (Johnson Family) have a hard time forgiving because we have been subliminally taught to shun people versus communicate our concerns. On the other hand, I believe that part of the road to forgiveness is for all parties involved to no longer repeat the same offenses.

Dee and I strive to start anew with revised family traditions. Dee read an Iyanla Vanzant quote which paraphrased said it is important to embrace change as we evolve in the twenty-first century. Too often, the older generation resists change like the plague. In an effort, to evolve, it's important for us to continue to push past prior barriers, traditions, and stereotypes. We should challenge older generations to think outside the box, but we must realize that it's a choice they have to make on their own. We cannot allow their views to hinder our process to start new traditions, values, and a way of life. However, the opposing view has been argued within our family, but one thing always holds true: "I've learned that people will forget what you said, people will forget what you did, but people will never forget how you made them feel" Dr. Maya Angelou.

Chapter 12

Breaking the Scheming Mindset

Most women find it calming to be able to speak to their in-laws about the one man they both love. I realized that I could not turn to Dee's parents for guidance with their son back in January of 2006. I received a call from Dee asking me to bail him out from Mecklenburg County Jail. I went to the county that morning around 4 a.m. and was told that I needed $1,750.00 to get him out. Prior to this incident, Dee and I were actively trying to purchase a house. Therefore, I was not spending any money to bail his ass out of jail. I turned to his parents, but when his father told me this was my responsibility, I lost it. In a nutshell, I let him know that Demetrius was not one of my children and my sole responsibilities are my two girls. I also informed Mr. Irick that it was his responsibility to guide his son, and he should continue to do so. When it came to his father trying to guide his son, you could not get anything out of him. Instead, the responsibility of teaching his son to be a man has rested on my shoulders. All I could think is this is not the role of a wife. I added that trying to guide his son is like going against the world; he challenges me with everything. Although, the purpose of my phone call seemed as if it were for financial assistance I was frustrated and needed to release my anger.

When it came to miniscule issues, his father provided details. Mr. Irick was able to tell me how to get a bail bondsman. He added that I would only be responsible for paying 10% of his bail. A plethora of information was provided about getting Dee out of trouble, but I received no assistance when trying to keep him on the right path. Once again, I stood alone with what felt like the weight of the world on my shoulders. Thankfully, no bond was needed just the signature of a responsible party. Demetrius called back to follow-up on my progress. I decided to let him sit there for a while to think about his actions. I signed Demetrius out 16 hours after being booked. Surprisingly, he expressed feelings of deep regret. However, this was only the beginning of his ordeal. Demetrius went to court and ended up with a revoked license for refusing to take the breathalyzer test the night he was stopped. I recall talking to his mother, and she suggested that Demetrius renew his South Carolina license. I immediately corrected her by saying he needs to fix the current issue not go around it by finding an escape. Needless to say, Demetrius renewed his South Carolina license.

About a month, or so later I told Dee I had a vision and advised him to find out from his lawyer how to get his license reinstated. My vision revealed that Demetrius was pulled over by a police officer. I saw this would result from his license plate being scanned by an officer driving behind his vehicle. A few weeks after my vision, I received a call from Demetrius which confirmed my dream. Another court date was scheduled and so I accompanied him since I was his designated driver. This became my role for many of Dee's work related travels, as well. I worked three 12 hour days (two day shifts, one overnight shift every Wednesday), went to class Monday through Thursday from 8:00 a.m. until 1:30 p.m. and was his designated driver in between. I later found out that Demetrius could have obtained a restricted license which could have prevented a lot of my long, stressful days.

This entire ordeal marked the downward spiral of our marriage. I was now married to a man who brought shame upon our family. Demetrius was someone that I felt would never get himself together. I was tired of being Demetrius' backbone without being able to depend on him in the same manner. After six years of marriage, I was starting to feel stagnant. For every step, I tried to take forward, I took two steps back. The devil resides with me, and he is hindering our household with the help of his buddy Demetrius Irick. I often asked what have I got myself into and how do I get myself, and the kids out. I was on the verge of surrendering all efforts but strong words from my sister's ex-boyfriend remain with me today: "Do what you have to do regardless of his actions. The entire household cannot fold for one person." I left Dee on his own to fix the mess he created. By February of 2007, he was able to get his NC license back. However, the expense of his DUI was just starting to kick in.

In March of 2007, I purchased a vehicle as a birthday gift to myself. Of course, the vehicle must be insured prior to driving off the lot. I switched my current insurance to the new vehicle. Once the insurance agent checked our driving records my insurance rate nearly doubled. Now I was being penalized for my husband's DUI. In addition, Demetrius was paying more than this to insure his own vehicle. Needless to say, we had to pay high premiums for three years. Times like this make me reflect on some words stated by my mother earlier in our marriage... "You ain't never gonna have anything with that boy." Sadly, I started to believe this to be true.

When we moved to Charlotte, Demetrius was so hungry and ready to start our life together that he accepted a job selling books and other odd items from business to business, person to person. As a once convicted felon, released from jail less than a year, Demetrius was limited to positions in the "general" ads like selling perfumes, daily paid labor, or commission-based jobs. Although he was eager to have some source of income, I temporarily deflated his ego by encouraging him to find a job with a set hourly rate. We both knew this option made better financial sense, than working long hours for a set daily pay. However, his criminal background would prove to make a simple choice very difficult. Demetrius filled out endless applications to no avail.

The answer to every felony conviction question was "Yes." I watched him leave the house motivated, only to return discouraged. A pep talk was necessary when he returned home from an interview which did not go so well. Our conversations involved me encouraging him to continue to try, do not give up, to trust that someone out there would give him a chance, and most of all, to be honest. Although I encouraged honesty, dishonesty proved to land Demetrius employment in his eyes. My fear with this dishonest approach was the potential for the ideal job to be taken from him once the lie was exposed. We struggled enough as it was. To pay for living a lie and to be stripped of our most important means of survival added more stress. If Dee continued down this path, I had no plans of staying in a marriage with no financial stability.

About two months after moving to Charlotte, Dee found a job in the electronics section of a department store. He was hired not only on his interview alone, but in spite of his response to the felony question. Dee only filled out applications that asked, "Have you been convicted of a felony within the past five years?" The difference with this question over asking, "Have you ever been convicted of a felony?" is "Yes" or "No." Of course, Dee accurately answered "No" to this question, and this gave him the image of a clean background. After all, his record was more than five years old, so nothing would show on record. In addition, some companies, as applied to this department store, did not always proceed with doing a criminal background check once "No" was circled. Demetrius had a stable job paying weekly, but we now faced another obstacle. He was paid on Friday, and by Monday, his check was spent.

Demetrius would exhaust his funds drinking beer, hanging with friends, or planning barbecues. This created problems and frustrations early within our relationship. After all the encouragement and in my mind a milestone conquered Demetrius added another twist to our problems. During this time, I discovered that he did not know how to save money and had never received an allowance, which could have taught him the concept of money. His credit was the worst I'd ever seen. I was only 23 and had a pretty good grasp on how to survive and be independent. I resented the days that my mother had my sister and I balancing a checkbook, while the other kids were outside playing. I thought my folks were nuts for talking about credit, because this conversation and the word "credit" meant absolutely nothing to me. Ha! How God works. Every message that I tried to ignore sunk in, because now I executed in my marriage what my parents taught me. Reiteration is definitely what children need. The message will never sink in if only stated once in a blue moon. Consistently modeling expectations and explaining the consequence for the wrong actions make a profound difference. In addition, constantly repeating and displaying these habits will prove to be most beneficial in the life of that child one day. After all, I never recall bill collectors calling my parents' house, only solicitors.

I could not understand why in 27 years this man had not learned how to run a household. I was truly confused, and I was angry with his parents for not instilling the independence he would need to support and lead a family. There were times that I grew tired of our long talks and my passion to encourage. My desire to push became overshadowed by degradation toward Dee. I was tired of the excuses. I wanted to see results and did not want to hear, "I have never been taught that" or "No one would hire me". I recall Dee believing that I lived a fairy tale life, acting as if our family had never been through struggles and referencing that we probably had received assistance from the system.

I was born and raised in New York. Surviving in a big city is totally different from life in a small country town. You are constantly on the grind to stay on top. The cost of living is more expensive than in a smaller town. Hence, my father worked six to seven days per week. I recall my mother being upset with my father because he worked so much and was absent from the home. Overall, my parents had a great relationship and were able to provide a solid foundation for my sister and me. We took annual vacations and most of all; my parents did things together, always showing a united front. My mother had a philosophy: "Where there is one, there is the other". Most importantly, my parents were consistent in their actions to provide a future for their children. Regardless of their differences from time to time, my parents did their part in the household. In time, Dee realized that my dad held down the fort and kept our family afloat with no outside assistance. Dee would grow to understand that this woman he married wants more out of life than a house and a car. I aspired to own a business one day, and Dee shared the same interests. When we first moved to Charlotte, Dee and I talked about owning a barber shop/hair salon since this concept did not exist in Charlotte. However, our dream never prospered beyond the conversation. Dee and I had issues within our relationship, and there was no way that any business would be formed right then. We were two individuals in a relationship going opposite directions.

One night we went to the grocery store to purchase a few items. After I had paid for the items, the cashier gave me back $10 too much in change. I immediately corrected the cashier and handed him back the excess change. The cashier was very grateful for my honesty and expressed how tired he was from working two jobs. I understood his position and felt even better about the decision I had made, knowing his negligence could cost the cashier his employment. Dee, on the other hand, was very upset and voiced his opinion once we got to the car. I would rather struggle than to keep any amount of money to aid our financial rut and later pay for the bad deed tenfold. Four years into our marriage and Dee still struggled with "stinking thinking".

There were times that Dee felt I picked him apart and found fault with his every move. He could not understand that I was passionate about his success and knew this man had what it took to live beyond his own expectations. Dee's past, along with the prejudices he faced as a felon seeking to find employment, caused him to be complacent. If Dee could find a stable job in the "labor" section of the classified ad and the company offered benefits, he was content. On the other hand, I was pushing Dee to apply for leadership positions in retail, knowing that his customer service skills and communication skills would make him an asset in this field. Dee often shied away from these positions due to fear of rejection and the repetition of telling the circumstances over and over and over again. Nonetheless, I saw a man with clouded dreams on a foggy road. I assumed that with some direction, Dee, would see clearer than when we first met. As years went by, I began to question my own sight. I wondered if the messages I tried to deliver were becoming wasted air. I recall one day, Dee and I were sitting inside our car talking to pass the time prior to his interview. In the rear view mirror, I noticed a woman nicely dressed in a suit exiting the building. As soon as she came through the door, she threw a long stream of spit to her left then proceeded to her car. I said to Dee, "Did you see how bad that looked?" He responded, "Yes, I never looked at it that way". I never had that problem with Dee spitting in public again. The message of looking the part and living the part is two different things. Dee finally got a chance to see that change starts from within if you seek to become a better individual. The manner in which you speak and act builds perception like the woman spitting in public.

I still tease Dee today about his management position at McDonalds. I enjoy throwing this job in his face, because he hated every day of the eight plus months he worked there. Since Dee had difficulty in retail, I encouraged him to find a position with a fast-food chain, because it could launch his career in the retail management field. I added that he would have to link the correlation during the interview once the time came. Demetrius Irick was not getting my perspective and told me that he would never flip burgers. We debated on this subject for a while until I reassured him that I would not steer him wrong. Needless to say, Dee filled out applications at three major food chains, but the golden arch was the only restaurant to accept his conviction. He was hired as an assistant manager, yet Demetrius was embarrassed about this job and shunned it. Almost every day that he went to work, I saw shame in his face. I reminded Dee that eventually people would no longer see a criminal before them, but instead a man with leadership experience. I told him to hold on long enough to get at least six months of experience. Dee's next position was a part-time front-end night shift supervisor. In this position, I noticed Demetrius become more confident in his ability, and he decided to apply for management positions in the retail industry. After almost 18 months of combined assistant management and supervisory experience on his resume, Dee was hired as an assistant manager of a well-known sneaker store. He worked there for over a year when he disclosed to me that he had lied on his application. I recall Dee later mentioning that he circled "No" on the application but later found his application in the stockroom on the shelf and changed it to "Yes". I felt so disappointed after Dee said he lied about his conviction. Dee never knew for certain if his manager found out, but her demeanor toward him definitely changed. Dee walked off the job after a year and a half of employment. Dee continued to circulate his resume until he came across a northern-based company looking to expand their business in the Southeast region. He told me about the company and was so full of excitement, but I had no clue what he was talking about. Dee felt that he had a great opportunity. He recalled me telling him to try with more northern-based companies, as I was confident that he would have more of a chance. On the other hand, a panel interview was a new and unfamiliar challenge. As always, this obstacle would be won, since I assisted with panel interviews at my place of employment and could provide the insight he needed. Needless to say, he was called for his second interview and was hired shortly after.

Demetrius "hit the floor running". I recall Dee sleeping in the store one night, because it took so long for the guys to finish varnishing the floor. In addition, he became responsible for managing two stores with minimal direction on how to handle one. For those who questioned how Demetrius got the position, I say he earned it with his determination, willingness to work long hours with hardly one day off per week for months (placing work before home another problem), and his continued efforts to prove himself. People fail to realize that you work hard from the first day you start and maintain that same consistency. Once you fail to display the work ethics that landed you the job in the beginning, you are making it easy to replace you. In other words, staff members terminate themselves due to poor work performance or behaviors which result in separation of employment.

In his role as a store manager, Dee was teaching his managers to be the person I desired my husband to be. Unfortunately, Dee was not quite where he needed to be, but I knew he would learn from his new position. I found it ironic some days, to hear Dee express his disappointment after exhausting so many efforts in coaching managers, he would later terminate for various reasons. I laughed to myself as I listened to him vent about some of the bad choices some of his people made. I thought about how much he sounded like me. I quickly reminded Dee that he had done some of the same things in his previous employment, and now God was showing him my frustrations through the actions of others. After all, I feel that, as a manager, you tend to hire people who have a little bit of yourself in them, whether past or present. With many of his managers, it was as if he held on to hope that they would change. I wish some of them knew how much he had their best interests at heart. If only some of them knew how passionate he was about giving them an opportunity he desired at their age. Demetrius wanted to give them the tools to be successful and to see them excel, if they so desired. Dee saw himself in some of his managers, and tried to guide them in a manner that could have worked best for him in his early 20's. The unfortunate reality

126

is that he was seeing the life he desired in some of his managers instead of seeing them as they were. Their lives were his past life. The better path Demetrius desired.

Everything that transpired within our relationship since 2000 stemmed from one problem area, finances. When I met Dee he had no idea about credit and how to manage bills. I was still naïve and minimized his lack of knowledge as something he chose not to do versus never been taught. This made no sense to me because I thought that everyone's parents did exactly what mine did as if there were a guide out there on parenting. I received an allowance whereas Dee received money on an as needed basis. My parents showed my sister and I how to manage a checkbook and how to write out our bills, but no one taught Dee this either. His lack of knowledge managing money handicapped him. Dee was unprepared for his role of leading a household and lacked the ability to take us to the next level. What seemed like common practices in the average household was foreign to my husband. We were totally opposite in every sense of the word. I was so frustrated at times with his parents for not taking the time to show Dee that my anger came across as a bash session towards him for not knowing. From the bash session, came the comparison between both sets of parents. Regardless, my tactics were ineffective, and the condescending comments had to stop. I finally realized that this dude seriously had no clue and I had the responsibility of teaching a 27 year old what I started learning at age 5. I second guessed my patience level with my role in this relationship. My role as the teacher became mentally draining because Dee was sometimes unwilling to make the necessary changes to get to the next level. He often resorted back to past habits of *getting over*, which resulted in us paying for it tenfold shortly after. In addition to our financial problems were Dee's unethical habits which infringed on our ability to save and live comfortably. Demetrius had a lot of hang ups and very little accountability for his actions. He was mad at the police for racial profiling and for pulling him over at random. I felt their actions were justifiable. A) Dee regularly checked his rear view mirrors while driving and seemed suspicious behind the wheel. B) Racial profiling proves to be effective in some cases because like Dee many are driving illegally. There were times when I felt like I bore the weight of Dee's world on my shoulders. I was not only trying to encourage better habits but had the task of pointing out the errors of his thought process and views. Demetrius' baggage became a turn off. Our issues began to overshadow the bond we were trying to build. Too much energy was exhausted in negative things, and that led to one thing - separation.

Chapter 13

Our Separation

I was very bitter about our separation but feeling stress free at the same time. While I knew that the separation was beneficial for both of us, I felt as if I had wasted time and energy trying to make something work that was never meant to be. In addition, my strongest hesitance for not walking away from the marriage sooner was Jaclyn. I did not want her to be without a father again. However, I had given up on our marriage by the seventh year. All our conversations were replaced by arguments. Our arguments became minimized by silence. I could go a month or more without speaking to Dee and no longer included him in the family meals. We were living separate lives and I was giving him my ass to kiss. Now I know why people say love is crazy.

I finally grew tired of the spending and the displeasure's. I wanted Demetrius to stay on the right path, but felt that he would never change. The burglary of our home in December 2009 was truly a turning point in our marriage. I faulted Dee for not properly camouflaging purchases he bought during the holiday. I was angry for him not being more adamant about properly securing our home and providing safety for his three ladies. In addition, I resented the idea of him parking his corporate vehicle with the company logo in front of our home. I felt we were sitting ducks, waiting to be robbed. After all, he purchased electronic giveaways for his stores, which were being stored in our home. In addition, the packing for our girls Wii and other household purchases were left by the curbside for anyone to see. Unsurprisingly, we enjoyed our new flat screen 40-inch television for about a week before we became victims of a breaking and entering. We lost two flat screen televisions, the girls' Wii unit and games, two laptops, a camcorder, two digital cameras, jewelry, cell phones, money and personal identification. Most of all, we were robbed of our security.

No one can understand the gravity of being victimized in this manner unless experienced first-hand. Although thanks to God no one was home, each day thereafter was like sleeping with one eye open. I was always fearful of our den door and never felt secure sitting in the den to watch television. Once hearing that our home was broken into, I knew that the persons had entered through our den door. Dee could never understand why I faulted him for this break-in, but I looked to him for security. I always feel that independent woman pay such a big cost for knowing how to hold their own. It is as if the man forgets how to treat the woman as just that. Nevertheless, this was an eye opener for me. No matter what I have, I must remain independent and do what is needed in our household.

Three months of insomnia, stress, and despair took a toll on my mind and body. I suffered from inexplicable body aches, severe headaches, and anxiety. I was slowly losing my mind and found it hard not to focus on the things that bothered me the most. While at work, I began to experience feelings of faintness; therefore, I knew it was time to remove myself from this situation. One day, my sister left work early to visit me in hopes of convincing me to stay with her for a while. She added, trying to hold back her tears, "I do not like seeing you this way. You have become a recluse, and that is not your personality. You need to get out for a while". I knew that Gayle was right and decided to pack my bags and stay with her. I never told Dee or the girls when or if I would return.

Sadly, the driving force of our separation was due to a ladder. I had asked Dee to secure the ladder on the ground against the back of the house before he left to go out of town. Instead, the ladder rested against the back of the house on our deck. I was concerned because the girls entered through the back door and could be hurt, as well. In addition, our dog was tied to the deck and could knock the ladder over and be injured as well. I left before him that Tuesday morning to return that evening with the ladder against the deck, with the top part of the deck split. This fueled me because, as usual, the man never took precautionary measures. Instead, he would pay for the outcome later.

I had enough of fixing what I considered his financial "fuck ups". I was so angry and tired that I did not realize I left the house for close to a month to live with my sister. When I returned, I ordered Dee to leave. I was tired of being ignored, and I was tired of him buying and spending with no regards. Dee managed to create $5,300 in expenses and showed no signs of cutting back. Dee's new corporate computer was damaged in less than two weeks of his company replacing the one that was stolen. Next, we were out shopping when Dee decided to stop at H.H. Gregg to "price" a laptop. I stayed in the car while he "just looked". The man returned with a laptop for himself and Jaclyn. The anger was marinating now. A few days later, I came home to see a Nikon camera, which he had purchased from a home shopping network, sitting on our table as well. This is the same place from which our flat screen was purchased just three months earlier. Lastly, he purchased an expensive ladder to clean out the gutters. Now, Dee is no handyman. Nonetheless, the gutters were hanging from the front of our house. The outer appearance of the house was the brink of my anxiety, and his reckless behavior was overboard. com.

In the midst of it all, the only legitimate spending was $2,700 to take down two trees and replace the gutters. By the time I started calculating all the expenses from December 2009 to March 2010, somebody had to go. I was too pissed to talk without my pressure rising. This man failed to include or inform me about any electronic item prior to purchase. I worked and brought home money as well, yet he purchased, while "we" paid for it. What the f— and I repeat, What the f— did he take me for? I was not going to stand for this bull another day. I felt that this marriage was no longer worth the stress, nor my mental health. I knew that I was taking a risk to separate our family but needed him to be on his own. Demetrius needed to take ownership of his financial mistakes with no one to back them. We agreed to separate for about six months and then discuss our plans to continue with a divorce or work on our marriage.

When Dee came to pick up the girls he stood at the front door. He did not come in nor did I invite him in. I no longer viewed him the same way. I felt as if I were seeing a stranger. I recall being down this road in a previous relationship. It's as if you look at the person, but you see a different face. I am truly disgusted and don't want to look at any man. "I am done son". After three months of separation and seeing how our divided family affected our girls, we made one last attempt to work on our marriage. While we both were taking one day at a time and making no promises, he became more involved in church and asked that I join him. After all, he attended this church for about two years before I stepped foot inside the doors. I did not trust that this change was real. I saw a man still living dishonestly and, most of all, disregarding his wife. Although my walk with God has nothing to do with his actions, I did not desire to do anything with Dee any longer. I had given up on us three years earlier.

Dee and I worked opposite each other, which for me was easier than dealing with the fact that we lived apart. Regardless of my actions or lack thereof, Dee became more involved in the church. The more he attended and ministered, the blatantly obvious his changes became to me. Dee was more loving, attentive, and respectful. He wanted us to devote an hour of our time reading or engaging in something productive for our relationship. Dee was more interested in learning about me again and getting our family back together. It was hard for him to get to this point because he resented me as I did him in the past. I now received a dose of my own medicine. A man who was so passionate about our family and this marriage had become wounded from the verbal abuse and degradation. I, on the other hand, was optimistic that this would come to pass, because I could see the change. Dee, however, was fueled by anger, resentment, and hurt, something I knew all too well. Regardless, of his feelings, Dee was still willing to try in hopes of rekindling the feelings he had attempted to bury.

We decided to move into his apartment, as the girls and I needed to get away from the same place that was burglarized. During the first month, I lived out of my suitcase. For the first time, I felt as if I did not belong. I was amazed at how much the décor of his apartment resembled things I would purchase. You would think a woman lived there. Although he always spoke of me in such high regard, I did not realize the influence I had until seeing his place. Living alone, he built confidence in his ability to be the leader of our house and the ability to stand independently.

So often, I felt that Dee leaned on me and would be unable to survive without me, without hitting rock bottom first. I knew that the only way for him to continue to understand his responsibility was if I did not assist with any bills within the apartment. After all, I was still paying the mortgage on the house. I bought the groceries as I did at the house, but let him know that I would not assist with any utilities. As time went on, I began to notice his stress level building. Dee was now concerned with how much money was "pissing in the wind". If we could afford to pay a mortgage and rent, we could deposit this money into our savings account each month or make the necessary repairs on our home to sell it.

During a recession, when people are losing their homes and struggling to come up with the money needed to pay the necessary bills, this man had been spending as if there were no tomorrow. I failed to understand why he lived this way and could not drill the concept of saving into his head after ten years of marriage. The separation taught him what I could not explain. As Dee always stated, "I learn better from experience". As this statement is true, I often tried to get him to follow my lead. I recall my mother telling me once, "There are some mistakes you cannot recover from, so it is best to listen to what people tell you". This statement was profound to me, because I thought about how some people's mistakes may have cost them their lives. Once again, I had to realize that Dee and I are two different people. I had to allow him to make his own mistakes at our expense.

We currently attend a marriage workshop at our church. In this workshop, we have learned to love and respect one another. We have learned the importance of communication and how the lack of it can strain a marriage. These simple things (showing love, giving respect, and openly communicating) are taken for granted in a marriage and create an unforeseen distance. The distance has now replaced by the desire to live apart. In a marriage that ends in divorce, not only does the husband and wife divorce, but the children will never have the same meaningful relationship that they once had when all lived under the same roof. This is impossible to obtain no matter how hard you try, because what seems right in a child's mind is their family residing together. Children don't truly understand why mommy and daddy live separate places. Witnessing firsthand the negative impact separation has on a child's psyche is enough. Living a life that can be a reflection and inspiration for others is not an easy task. Learning what it is to be a Christian and living a positive life is a constant work in progress.

The separation, hearing our children openly discussing their feelings and the toll that it had on both myself and Dee made me realize that we had to change. In order for us to continue being married, we had to start over and apply new principles to our marriage. I thought back to something a young lady said during an interview at "Big Brother, Big Sister". She said, "Two parents can be more dysfunctional than one". As I reflect on my life as a single parent, Jaclyn did not have to deal with challenges of two parents feuding or two philosophies trying to be formed into one rule. However, within a marriage, the most challenging obstacle is getting two people on one accord. Hence, being on one accord with my parents and sister in regard to raising Jaclyn was easy; we had similar views. Starting your life anew with someone of a different upbringing can be difficult. My daughter had everything she needed and was showered with love from my parents, my sister, and her mother. Jaclyn was a happy baby. I look at her today with hurt in her eyes and wondered why after 13 years Jaclyn sought to find her biological father. I felt that she was more inquisitive about him as a result of my separation from Dee. In my eyes, I felt that my daughter began to lose her sense of where she belonged. If we legally separated, the courts would only provide support for Daijah, which would also create an emotional divide between our children. Daijah on the other hand, had both her parents, but the father she is so attached to, Mommy put out. In addition, Daijah does not understand why my parents cannot live with us. She would state to my mom, "I want us to live in the same house". She added, "Why can't we live in the same house?" Daijah's perception of the family is everyone living together. Daijah wanted to have everyone she loved under one roof; her big heart reminded me so much of her father's.

Daijah reminds me of Dee in many ways. She is quiet, very forgiving, loves hard, and sees no evil. If Daijah feels that a minor disagreement between Dee and me could result in an argument, she intervenes and provides her perspective. In addition, Daijah is analytical and will only speak when comfortable with your being, a quality she obtained from her mother. Jaclyn is outspoken, outgoing, a born leader, and will not back down from anything. The girl is a mini-me. Some days I laugh to myself when I see our children, because the older they get, the more I see how our behaviors influence their lives in a mighty way. They both are great communicators, and they both are very receptive to their surroundings. Jaclyn and Daijah have really good writing skills and will not hesitate to verbalize what they feel. Dee and I both instill effective communication in our girls, since we were raised in totally opposite environments.

Children have such an innate ability to be strong in times when their parents are weak. My then, 13-year-old told me that chasing a paycheck is not worth losing time with your family. I knew this statement was directed toward me. I did not take Jaclyn's comment personally, as I realized that she is right and that I need to spend more time with our children. Since attending school back in 2006, and since the problems within our marriage, my presence in the home became minimal. I took the girls shopping with me after work a short time ago, and once home, my 9-year-old said, "At least we got to spend time with you, since you are always working". Children can recognize a problem and know the right things to say in their attempts to nurture you, as we once did them in their infancy stage. The actions of my 9-year-old and the despair on my 13-year-old's face made me realize that we need to maintain a healthy environment for our children at all times. In the midst of our arguments, back lashing, and a house divided, our children suffered heavily. We now owe it to the children as well as ourselves to work together, build, and keep the family together.

Today, Demetrius is a successful District Manager of the South and North Carolina regions of a popular urban men's wear store. He has ministered to men in prison for over two years. Demetrius Irick is a great father, a better husband and provider, the leader of our household, role model, and most of all, a man of God. In a world where so many people view criminals all the same and are unwilling to give one a chance; Demetrius surpassed the expectations of many. The motto I live by and encourage my family to follow: "Live to exceed the stereotypes and expectations of others".

Although, our families still have barriers that hinder them from connecting, Dee and I continue our efforts in linking the divide. In addition, we started hosting our annual Johnson-Irick family reunion. We established the reunion with the intent to bring our families together and allow our children to bond with their siblings. The family reunion was a blast; however, one disappointment was our inability to get my mother's relatives to attend. There is such a breakdown in communication amongst my mother's siblings that tempers flare over the least things said.

Also, the reluctance for them to move on from the past still continues. Shamefully I admit that these behaviors have been passed down. For this reason, I have learned to calm my tongue and not allow things beyond my control to alter my temperament. I let go and let God which has brought more peace in my life.

Unfortunately, Mr. and Mrs. Irick and I still have a distance which has now extended to the man we all love. Our conversations are guarder as we all try to be mindful of what we say. In retrospect, our past deeds still dictate what could be. Yet, I have learned through our marital separation that the lack of communication can be detrimental to any relationship. In my ideal world, when two people get married both families would unite as one. We would have annual gatherings over Sunday dinner and do family building activities. If we all were willing to understand and respect each other's views and equally work towards change, our relationships could grow. Old habits are meant to be broken as nothing should remain the same.

There have been recent changes in my parents, to include my mother going to my in-laws house in support of Kamon's (nephew-in-law) high school graduation party. In addition, my parents and sister showed a united front in attendance at Kamon's graduation, and the families sat together as one. We laughed and joked with one another like old times. Although, we still have a degree of distance, children have a way of bringing family together; even if short lived.

A majority of our time and efforts are invested in bonding with our children, to include our nephew

Kamon. Kamon has stayed with us off and on during spring, summer breaks and winter breaks since he was 10 years old. He is the son I may not have the opportunity to give birth to (too old and unwilling to start over), a big brother and positive inspiration to both Jaclyn and Daijah. At age 18, Kamon's trials and quiet observations have taught him what not to do. Just as we have done with Kamon, we will continue to be the voice and positive influence in the lives of all our nephews; to help mold another productive male in society. Sometimes all we need is one voice along with constant reinforcement to make the difference. As Kamon enters college this fall, we will continue to provide the direction he will need until he can stand alone.

At a time when our future together seemed so bleak, Dee and I work harder today at committing ourselves to a lifelong relationship. Dee and I take quarterly vacations; two as a family and two without the children. Every Wednesday is our date night to have private time alone as we did when we first met. This time is spent learning each other again and peeling off more layers from previous years. Although adults find it difficult to iron out their differences, once again, the children suffer. If we fail to connect and bond with one another, our children are robbed of having a healthy relationship or knowing their extended family. In essence, we allow our differences to create a divide that deteriorates a family. The result is a unified family during death versus actively engaging and providing support during a joyous time.

God's Intervention

By Demetrius

Chapter 14

My Walk with God

As I sit and reflect on the goodness of our God, the thought of His power and grace brings me to tears. I think back to my breakdown and realize, my transition was the intent of Gods purpose; to use me. I realize now that my worldly mind wasn't ready for the spiritual intervention God was taking me through. I truly believe my grandmother's death was an eye-opener for me. I felt that her life was taken to allow me the benefit of living my life with purpose. I was walking around lost, on the fast track to death. I cannot recount all of the times God has intervened on my behalf, but from my reflections, I have decided to share with you the following:

- Car Wreck: During my mental transition, I drove a car speeding approximately 90 miles per hour. I overcorrected which cause the vehicle to careen off the road. All passengers were ejected to include my brother, his two friends and me. The car was totaled, yet we all walked away with minor scratches and bruises.

- Bullet nearly grazed by head: I was sitting in the center of the back seat when shots were fired into the vehicle.

- I was jumped by members of a well-known street gang and dealers from out of town, known as the "Florida Boys". They circled around me with their weapons drawn. One member standing behind me hit me with a gun in the back of my head. Although, they had the opportunity to kill me, badly beaten, I walked away.

- There were several nights that I did so much cocaine that I should not have survived. My heart would beat so fast. In addition, the cocaine started to play vicious mind games. I began to see cocaine everywhere on the streets, confused it for the lint in my pockets, and on the dollar bills used to snort it.

- Feeling out of control and as if my life had no meaning, I tried to commit suicide. However, God showed me the sign I asked for to convince me that he had a plan.

Today, I am confident that God saved and protected me for a reason. Today, I live my life with purpose. My purpose is to tell people of the goodness and glory of our Lord and Savior Jesus Christ. My life experiences are my testimony to share with others in hopes that *someone* will avoid the same pitfalls. I committed enough evil to last two lifetimes, and it is time that I put positive energy back into the world. I yearn for that feeling of completeness I get from helping others. Through mentoring, I help others, and I am rewarded with so much more in return that I cannot even put a price tag on the giving.

Closing Comments from a Loving Husband and a Loving Wife

Dee:

As I stated when I first started this book, I hope that you find your path. I hope that you use this book as inspiration to do something better with your life. I hope that as you read the contents, something jumps out to you that you can use to help another soul. It is my sincerest aspiration that if you get nothing else out of this book, you will understand that God is real. I hope that you will understand that He will never leave you or forsake you, no matter what you think and feel right this minute. If you decide to give your life over to Jesus and you are sincere in your heart and soul, he will make a difference in your life.

Thank you for purchasing our book. I sincerely hope that you were able to take from my life experiences a way to do more with the life you have. I don't want you to make excuses but to push past your shortcomings and reach your full potential. I hope that this book can inspire young kids to stay away from drugs and violence and open a dialogue between parents and children. Parents, control the use of social media. Don't let Facebook, B.E.T, VH1, MTV, or other media outlets influence your kids and teach them the things they need to learn in life. It is so important for us as parents to lay the foundation for our children. Please talk to your kids about sex, drugs, gangs, school, their dreams, and your desires for their lives. As parents, we should inspire them to greatness and encourage them to do more with their lives on a constant basis. Parents, speak life into your children's spirits.

I hope you can use my experiences to help either yourself or a loved one overcome similar obstacles. I hope this book will be used as an inspiration and motivation to all. I hope that as you read about these experiences, you are able to find similarities that can help identify potential issues. Please use those similarities to help our youth avoid a similar path. It is my sincerest desire that the terrible experiences that I have gone through will motivate and encourage other young men to make better choices and push parents to listen to their children. I hope that young adults will use this book to listen to their parents, pastors, or mentors in their lives. I hope that the children who do not have any mentors use these experiences to guide them and minister to their souls to avoid the same fate. Please reach out to me and tell me what you enjoyed best about the book and what you would like to see in the next book.

My Prayer

It is my prayer that everyone who doesn't know the Lord Jesus will give or rededicate his or her life to the Lord after reading this book. I hope the situations and examples will inspire all to greatness. I pray, Father, that You will move Your Spirit upon the readers of these pages, the hearts of our children, and the parents. I pray for the young girls and women, that You will give them strength to be self-sufficient and respectful of their bodies and minds. I pray that You will strengthen them as they take on the burden of raising our boys to men. I pray for our teenage boys and men who haven't quite gotten to where they want to be but who are willing and open to making the necessary changes to get there. I pray You will fill them with motivation and direction so they can reach the goals you have placed in their being. Father, I pray for the world and this generation. I pray that we never forget who You are and what our true purpose in this life is. I pray we never forget that this life is temporary and, ultimately, we should be working to save souls and fighting the good fight to bring our lost to You. In Jesus' name I pray… Amen.

Jacqueline:

In conclusion, never hesitate to help, inspire, or motivate another person. We all at some point in our lives will become lost souls seeking guidance.

Part of life's journey is the trials, tribulations, and circumstances that God intends for us to undergo in order to become better individuals. In the midst of our mess, we must continue to praise Him, because the test will be over and the victory will be yours to claim; thanks to His mercy. We should never lie down in the midst of our hardships, but instead find that inner strength to keep moving until we get to that finish line. We hold the key to our success, and our most detrimental roadblock is the one we create for ourselves: EXCUSES!

A Letter from Jaclyn

I have wanted to be an actress since the age of six. I imagined myself growing up to be a well-known television star. Reality finally hit at the age of thirteen. I learned about entrepreneurship in my AVID (Advanced Via Individual Determination) program at school. The word "entrepreneurship" inspired my career decision.

My dream now is to open a school of arts and teach young kids like myself the arts of drama. I believe in being my own boss. I don't believe in people telling me what I have to do just to make money. Everyone should always have the opportunity to think on their own. Everyone is unique, but we all are too afraid to be open with it. I want to teach kids that it's okay to be different and open-minded. I have struggled with this for a while. People love to laugh and pick on the kid that stands out, but they never stop to think about that person's feelings. What if everyone in the world looked the same? What if only one color existed? What if everyone in the world had the same outfit in their closets? The world would be a boring place. When you copy others, you are taking bits away from your own personality to make it like someone else's. Forget about the rude comments people make when it comes to you and your personality. They are just another boring soul waiting to be released.

A Letter from Daijah

Later on in life, I want to open my own fashion design company. I have always liked doing creations for my dolls. I use the dolls as practice, because I know if I keep trying and working harder, one day I might get to open a company. I will eventually get paid to do what I truly enjoy. I like to design clothes because it's fun and gives me something to do when I am bored. It keeps me busy, and it also shows me some ideas of how to better my creations in the future.

I love that my mommy plays with my sister and me, and even when she is tired from her work, she still finds time for us. She is so caring, loving, and playful. My daddy likes to spend alone time with my sister and me when he is not out of town or working. I love that my dad jokes around, plays, and has fun with my sister and me. My daddy makes sure that we read and do something constructive all the time. My sister is nice, and we are close. We do almost everything together. She plays with me a lot and forgives me when I do something wrong.

I want our family to continue to go through the Bible as much as we can. We all need to gain a better relationship with God, because no one is 100% holy. I have learned not to get mad at my parents when I have done something wrong and they have to punish me for something I did. My parents make it easy for me to understand my actions, why I was wrong, and to make better choices. I love that my family loves me.

A Letter from Kamon

As the child, of two young parents', I learned a couple of valuable lessons about life in my early youth. I felt there were two options: fall victim to my parents' situations or learn from them and apply the knowledge to my everyday actions. My mom was 18 and my dad was 16 at the time I was born. My father is hardly involved, but at least I can say I know him. However, knowing of him but not having a meaningful relationship with him hurts more. My mother, a single parent, has worked to provide for my brothers and I. Just as my uncle Dee, we were born of modest means, but the love and support of family (grandparents, aunts, uncles and other relatives) helped. At times, I feel like such a burden on both my parents and relatives who step up in their place.

There has been numerous occasions where I wanted to do the wrong things. Whenever I am in such a position, I always ask myself, "How would this affect my future?" If I think it would have a negative impact on my future then that is the flashing red light indicating that I should not get involved. I also keep myself on track by surrounding myself with people who are already successful or as hungry for success as I am. Watching those who are already successful helps me to remember that it is possible to achieve your goals. I aspire one day to be a successful architect. My definition of success is when I reach a point where I am financially stable, content with life, and able to give back. As many would limit their expectations of what I can achieve, I should not be defined by my parents' mistakes. As I prepare for college in the fall, I hope I will continue to apply all I have learned. If you are in the same or similar situation remember- you are the only one that stands in the way of your success. Lastly, try not to worry about how others view you, but more importantly how you see yourself.

Appendix

Faith without works is dead. Get in the game; don't sit by and watch your children self-destruct and do nothing. Be fearless in your attempts to change and better their lives. Your consistent message and example is needed and will be appreciated later in life. It is important to understand, parents, that when someone uses drugs, over time it alters the brain. In some cases, it even alters the way the individual's brain looks and functions. It is these changes in the brain that interfere with the way a person thinks, the way he exercises judgment, good or bad. It makes them feel that it's normal to use these drugs, although they know it's not good for them. These changes are also part of the reason why the individual has the cravings, and they make the need to have them powerful. Common signs and symptoms of drug abuse can be found at the American Council for Drug Education's Web site: www.acde.org/parent/signs.htm.

SIGNS AND SYMPTOMS OF DRUG USE

It is important to keep in mind that if a child shows any of the following symptoms, it does not necessarily mean that he or she is using drugs. The presence of some of these behaviors could be the product of adolescent stress. Others may be symptoms of depression or a host of other problems. Whatever the cause, they may warrant attention, especially if they persist or if they occur in a cluster. A mental health professional or a caring and concerned adult may help a youngster successfully overcome a crisis and develop more effective coping skills, often preventing further problems.

The key is change; it is important to watch for any significant changes in your child's physical appearance, personality, attitude or behavior.

Physical Signs

- Loss of appetite, increase in appetite, any changes in eating habits, unexplained weight loss or gain
- Slowed or staggering walk; poor physical coordination
- Inability to sleep, awake at unusual times, unusual laziness
- Red, watery eyes; pupils larger or smaller than usual; blank stare

- Cold, sweaty palms; shaking hands
- Puffy face, blushing or paleness
- Smell of substance on breath, body or clothes.
- Extreme hyperactivity; excessive talkativeness
- Runny nose; hacking cough
- Needle marks on lower arm, leg or bottom of feet
- Nausea, vomiting or excessive sweating
- Tremors or shakes of hands, feet or head
- Irregular heartbeat.

Behavioral Signs

- Change in overall attitude/personality with no other identifiable cause
- Changes in friends; new hang-outs; sudden avoidance of old crowd; doesn't want to talk about new friends; friends are known drug users
- Change in activities or hobbies
- Drop in grades at school or performance at work; skips school or is late for school
- Change in habits at home; loss of interest in family and family activities.
- Difficulty paying attention; forgetfulness
- General lack of motivation, energy, self-esteem, "I don't care" attitude.
- Sudden oversensitivity, temper tantrums, or resentful behavior
- Moodiness, irritability, or nervousness
- Silliness or giddiness

- Paranoia
- Excessive need for privacy; unreachable
- Secretive or suspicious behavior
- Car accidents
- Chronic dishonesty
- Unexplained need for money, stealing money or items
- Change in personal grooming habits
- Possession of drug paraphernalia

Drug Specific Symptoms:

Marijuana: Glassy, red eyes; loud talking and inappropriate laughter followed by sleepiness; a sweet burnt scent; loss of interest, motivation; weight gain or loss

Alcohol: Clumsiness; difficulty walking; slurred speech; sleepiness; poor judgment; dilated pupils; possession of a false ID card

Depressants: (including barbiturates and tranquilizers) Seems drunk as if from alcohol but without the associated odor of alcohol; difficulty concentrating; clumsiness; poor judgment; slurred speech; sleepiness; and contracted pupils

Stimulants: Hyperactivity; euphoria; irritability; anxiety; excessive talking followed by depression or excessive sleeping at odd times; may go long periods of time without eating or sleeping; dilated pupils; weight loss; dry mouth and nose

Inhalants: (Glues, aerosols, and vapors) Watery eyes; impaired vision, memory and thought; secretions from the nose or rashes around the nose and mouth; headaches and nausea; appearance of intoxication; drowsiness; poor muscle control; changes in appetite; anxiety; irritability; an unusual number of spray cans in the trash

Hallucinogens: Dilated pupils; bizarre and irrational behavior including paranoia, aggression, hallucinations; mood swings; detachment from people; absorption with self or other objects, slurred speech; confusion

Heroin: Needle marks; sleeping at unusual times; sweating; vomiting; coughing and sniffling; twitching; loss of appetite; contracted pupils; no response of pupils to light

Tobacco/Nicotine: Smell of tobacco; stained fingers or teeth

(Taken from the American Council for Drug Education: http://www.acde.org/parent/signs.htm)

Information for the Orangeburg Massacre of 1968: http://www.orangeburgmassacre1968.com